# General Explanations
# of the
# Administration's Fiscal Year 2010
# Revenue Proposals

Department of the Treasury
May 2009

# Table of Contents[1]

[1] The Administration's primary policy proposals reflect changes from a tax baseline that modifies current law by "patching" the alternative minimum tax, freezing the estate tax, and making permanent a number of the tax cuts enacted in 2001 and 2003.  The baseline changes to current law are described in the Appendix.  In some cases, the policy descriptions in the body of this report make note of the baseline (e.g., descriptions of upper-income tax provisions), but elsewhere the baseline is implicit.

# TAX CUTS FOR FAMILIES AND INDIVIDUALS

## PROVIDE THE "MAKING WORK PAY" CREDIT

### Current Law

In 2009 and 2010, individual taxpayers are eligible for a refundable tax credit of 6.2 percent of earned income up to a maximum credit of $400 ($800 for joint filers). Thus, workers receive a credit on the first $8,065 of earned income ($16,130 for joint filers). The credit phases out at a rate of 2 percent for taxpayers with modified adjusted gross income in excess of $75,000 ($150,000 for joint filers). Dependent filers are not eligible for the credit. Neither the maximum credit amount nor the beginning of the phase-out range is indexed for inflation.

The IRS withholding schedules are modified to reflect the Making Work Pay (MWP) credit, with reconciliation of overwithholding and underwithholding on annual income tax returns.

### Reasons for Change

The MWP credit partially offsets the regressivity of the Social Security payroll tax. It effectively raises the income of workers eligible for the credit, which encourages individuals to enter the labor force. Permanency and indexing the beginning of the phase-out range for inflation would ensure that workers continue to receive some of the benefits of the credit and low-income workers continue to receive a work incentive. In addition, the MWP credit could be extended to more people by raising the phase-out range.

The MWP credit contributes to the high marginal tax rates faced by workers in the phase-out range. Lowering the phase-out rate would produce fewer distortions.

### Proposal

The proposal would make the MWP credit permanent and index the beginning of the phase-out range for inflation. In addition, the phase-out rate would be reduced to 1.6 percent.

The proposal is effective for tax years beginning after December 31, 2010.

**EXPAND THE EARNED INCOME TAX CREDIT (EITC):  PROVIDE MARRIAGE PENALTY RELIEF AND ENHANCED BENEFITS FOR LARGER FAMILIES**

## Current Law

Low and moderate-income workers may be eligible for a refundable earned income tax credit (EITC).  Eligibility for the EITC is based on the presence and number of qualifying children in the worker's household, adjusted gross income (AGI), earned income, investment income, filing status, age, and immigration and work status in the United States.  The amount of the EITC is based on the presence and number of qualifying children in the worker's household, AGI, earned income, and filing status.

The EITC has a phase-in range (where each additional dollar of earned income results in a larger credit), a maximum range (where additional dollars earned or AGI have no effect on the size of the credit), and a phase-out range (where each additional dollar of the larger of earned income or AGI results in a smaller total credit).  The EITC for childless workers is much smaller and phases out at a lower income level than does the EITC for workers with qualifying children.  The EITC is larger for workers with more qualifying children, reaching a maximum amount at three qualifying children.  The phase-out range for joint filers begins at a higher income level than for an individual with the same number of qualifying children who files as a single filer or as a head of household. The width of the phase-in range and the beginning of the phase-out range are indexed for inflation.  Hence, the maximum amount of the credit and the end of the phase-out range are effectively indexed.  The following chart summarizes the EITC for 2009.

| | Childless Taxpayers | Taxpayers with Qualifying Children | | |
| --- | --- | --- | --- | --- |
| | | One Child | Two Children | Three or More |
| Phase-in rate | 7.65% | 34.00% | 40.00% | 45.00% |
| Minimum earnings for maximum credit | $5,970 | $8,950 | $12,570 | $12,570 |
| Maximum credit | $457 | $3,043 | $5,028 | $5,657 |
| Phase-out rate | 7.65% | 15.98% | 21.06% | 21.06% |
| Phase-out begins | $7,470 ($12,470 joint) | $16,420 ($21,420 joint) | $16,420 ($21,420 joint) | $16,420 ($21,420 joint) |
| Phase-out ends | $13,440 ($18,440 joint) | $35,463 ($40,463 joint) | $40,295 ($45,295 joint) | $43,279 ($48,279 joint) |

To be eligible for the EITC, workers may have a maximum of $3,100 of investment income. (This amount is indexed for inflation.)

In 2009 and 2010, the beginning of the phase-out range for joint filers is $5,000 higher than for other filers.  (The amount will be indexed in 2010.)   Under current law, beginning in 2011 the EITC for workers with the same number of qualifying children will phase-out over the same income range regardless of filing status.  Under the assumption that certain provisions of the

Economic Growth and Tax Relief Reconciliation Act of 2001 (EGTRRA) are made permanent, the additional $5,000 for married filers will revert in 2011 to $3,000 indexed from 2007.

In 2009 and 2010, the EITC phases in at a faster rate for workers with three or more qualifying children than for workers with two qualifying children (45 and 40 percent, respectively). The accelerated phase-in rate results in a higher credit and a longer phase-out range. This provision expires after 2010, at which point workers with three or more qualifying children will receive the same EITC as similarly situated workers with two qualifying children.

## Reasons for Change

The beginning of the phase-out range for joint filers is higher than for other workers with the same number of qualifying children in order to reduce the "EITC marriage penalty." This marriage penalty occurs because the income of both spouses is counted toward eligibility for joint filers, but the income of only the "head of household" filer is considered if the individuals are not married. Extending marriage penalty relief improves fairness and removes financial impediments to marriage for some low-income households.

Families with many children face larger expenses related to raising their children than do smaller families and as a result have higher poverty rates. The steeper phase-in rate and larger maximum credit for workers with three or more qualifying children helps them meet their expenses while maintaining work incentives.

## Proposal

The proposal would make permanent the $5,000 (indexed) increase in the beginning of the phase-out range for joint filers relative to other individuals.

Furthermore, the proposal would make permanent the expansion of the EITC for workers with three or more qualifying children. Specifically, the phase-in rate of the EITC for workers with three or more qualifying children under the American Recovery and Reinvestment Act of 2009 (ARRA) would be maintained at 45 percent, resulting in a higher maximum credit amount and longer phase-out range.

The proposal would be effective for tax years beginning after December 31, 2010.

# EXPAND THE REFUNDABILITY OF THE CHILD TAX CREDIT: MAKE PERMANENT THE $3,000 EARNINGS THRESHOLD AND ELIMINATE INDEXING

## Current Law

An individual may claim a $1,000 tax credit for each qualifying child. A qualifying child must meet the following four tests:

(1) Relationship – The child generally must be the taxpayer's son, daughter, grandchild, sibling, niece, nephew, or foster child.

(2) Residence – The child must live with the taxpayer in the same principal place of abode for over half the year.

(3) Support – The child must not have provided more than half of his or her own support.

(4) Age – The child must be under the age of 17.

For purposes of the child tax credit, a qualifying child must be a citizen, national, or resident of the United States. The child tax credit is phased out for individuals with income over certain thresholds,[1] and is partially refundable.

In 2009 and 2010, individuals may be eligible for a refundable amount (the additional child tax credit) equal to the lesser of 15 percent of earned income in excess of $3,000 and any child credit unclaimed due to insufficient tax liability.[2] Under the assumption that certain provisions of EGTRRA are made permanent, in 2011 the earned income threshold reverts to an amount indexed from $10,000 in 2000.

Families with three or more children may determine the additional child tax credit using an alternative formula based on the extent to which a taxpayer's social security taxes exceed the taxpayer's EITC.

## Reasons for Change

Because the wages of low-income families have failed to keep up with inflation, continued indexing will result in a decreasing number of low-income families able to take advantage of the credit each year and smaller credits for the families who receive the credit.

---

[1] Specifically, the otherwise allowable child tax credit is reduced by $50 for each $1,000 (or fraction thereof) of modified adjusted gross income over $75,000 for single individuals or heads of households, $110,000 for married individuals filing joint returns, and $55,000 for married individuals filing separate returns.

[2] Earned income for purposes of the refundable amount is defined as the sum of wages, salaries, tips, and other taxable employee compensation plus net self-employment earnings to the extent that these amounts are included when computing taxable income.

Furthermore, if the threshold increases to $12,700 in 2011 as scheduled, an estimated 11 million low-income families would have a tax increase as a result.

## Proposal

The proposal would make permanent the $3,000 earnings threshold for refundability of the child credit. In addition the earnings threshold would no longer be indexed for inflation.

The proposal would be effective for tax years beginning after December 31, 2010.

## EXPAND THE SAVER'S CREDIT AND PROVIDE FOR AUTOMATIC ENROLLMENT IN IRAS

### Expand the Saver's Credit

### Current Law

A nonrefundable tax credit is available for eligible individuals who make voluntary contributions to 401(k) plans and other retirement plans, including IRAs. The maximum annual contribution eligible for the credit is $4,000 for married couples filing jointly and $2,000 for single taxpayers or married individuals filing separately, resulting in maximum credits of $2,000 and $1,000, respectively. The credit rate is 10 percent, 20 percent or 50-percent, depending on the taxpayer's adjusted gross income (AGI) (the amount of which is adjusted each calendar year based on the cost-of-living adjustment). In 2009, "eligible individuals" who may claim the credit are

- Married couples filing jointly with incomes up to $55,500;
- Heads of households with incomes up to $41,625; and
- Married individuals filing separately and singles with incomes up to $27,750,

who are 18 or older, other than individuals who are full-time students or claimed as a dependent on another taxpayer's return.

The credit is available with respect to an eligible individual's "qualified retirement savings contributions." These include (i) elective deferrals to a section 401(k) plan, section 403(b) plan, section 457 plan, SIMPLE, or simplified employee pension (SEP); (ii) contributions to a traditional or Roth IRA; and (iii) other voluntary employee contributions to a qualified retirement plan, including voluntary after-tax contributions and voluntary contributions to a defined benefit pension plan. The eligible individual may direct that the amount of any refund attributable to the credit may be directly deposited by the IRS into an IRA or certain other accounts.

The credit is nonrefundable and, therefore, offsets regular tax liability or minimum tax liability. The credit is in addition to any deduction or exclusion that would otherwise apply with respect to the contribution.

### Reason for Change

The saver's credit should be amended to more effectively encourage moderate- and lower-income individuals to save for retirement. Because it is currently nonrefundable, the saver's credit only offsets a taxpayer's income tax liability and therefore gives no saving incentive to tens of millions of households without income tax liability. In addition, the current three-tier credit rate structure should be simplified, the eligibility income threshold should be raised to increase the number of households eligible for the credit, and the credit rate should be increased for most eligible households. Finally, making the saver's credit more like a matching contribution would enhance the likelihood that the credit would be saved and would increase the salience of the incentive by framing it as a match similar to the familiar employer matching contributions to 401(k) plans.

## Proposal

The proposal would make the saver's credit fully refundable and would provide for the credit to be deposited automatically in the qualified retirement plan account or IRA to which the eligible individual contributed. Making the saver's credit more like a matching contribution would enhance the likelihood that the credit would be saved and would increase the salience of the incentive by framing it as a match similar to the familiar employer matching contributions to 401(k) plans. The proposal would offer a meaningful saving incentive to tens of millions of additional households while simplifying the current three-tier credit structure and raising the eligibility income threshold to cover millions of additional moderate-income taxpayers.

In place of the current 10-percent/20-percent/50-percent credit for qualified retirement savings contributions up to $2,000 per individual, the proposal would match 50-percent of such contributions up to $500 per individual (indexed annually for inflation beginning in taxable year 2011). The eligibility income threshold would be increased to $65,000 for married couples filing jointly, $48,750 for heads of households, and $32,500 for singles and married individuals filing separately, with the amount of savings eligible for the credit phased out at a 5-percent rate for AGI exceeding those levels.

The proposal would be effective December 31, 2010.

## Automatic Enrollment in IRAS

## Current Law

A number of tax-preferred, employer-sponsored retirement savings programs exist under current law. These include section 401(k) cash or deferred arrangements, section 403(b) programs for public schools and charitable organizations, section 457 plans for governments and nonprofit organizations, and simplified employee pensions and SIMPLE IRAs for small employers. Individuals who do not have access to an employer-sponsored retirement saving arrangement may be eligible to make smaller tax-favored contributions to individual retirement accounts or individual retirement annuities (IRAs).

IRA contributions are limited to $5,000 a year (plus $1,000 for those age 50 or older). Section 401(k) plans permit contributions (employee plus employer contributions) of up to $49,000 a year (of which $16,500 can be pre-tax employee contributions) plus $5,500 of additional pre-tax employee contributions for those age 50 or older.

## Reasons for Change

For many years, until the current recession, the personal saving rate in the United States has been exceedingly low. In addition, tens of millions of U.S. households have not placed themselves on a path to become financially prepared for retirement, and the proportion of U.S. workers participating in employer-sponsored plans has remained stagnant for decades at no more than about half the total work force notwithstanding repeated private-sector and congressional attempts to expand coverage. Participation in employer-sponsored retirement saving plans such as 401(k) plans typically has ranged from two thirds to three quarters of eligible employees, but making saving easier by making it automatic has been shown to be remarkably effective at boosting participation. Automatic enrollment in 401(k) plans (enrolling employees by default unless they opt out) has tended to increase participation to more than 9 out of 10 eligible employees. In contrast, for workers who lack access to a retirement plan at their workplace and are eligible to engage in tax-favored retirement saving by taking the initiative and making the decisions required to establish and contribute to an IRA, the IRA participation rate tends to be less than 1 out of 10.

Numerous employers, especially those with smaller or lower-wage work forces, have been reluctant to adopt a retirement plan for their employees, in part out of concern about their ability to afford the cost of making employer contributions or the per-capita cost of complying with tax-qualification or ERISA (Employee Retirement Income Security Act) requirements. These employers could help their employees save -- without employer contributions or plan qualification or ERISA compliance -- simply by making their payroll systems available as a conduit for regularly transmitting employee contributions to an employee's IRA. Such "payroll deduction IRAs" could build on the success of workplace-based payroll-deduction saving by using the excess capacity to promote saving that is inherent in employer payroll systems, especially those that use automatic enrollment. However, despite efforts a decade ago by Treasury, the IRS, and the Department of Labor to approve and promote the option of payroll deduction IRAs, few employers have adopted them or even are aware that this option exists.

Accordingly, requiring employers that do not sponsor any retirement plan (and that are above a certain size) to make their payroll system available to employees and automatically enroll them in IRAs could achieve a major breakthrough in retirement saving coverage. Many employers may then be more willing to take the next step and adopt an employer plan (permitting much greater tax-favored employee contributions than an IRA plus the option of employer contributions). In addition, the process of saving and choosing investments could be simplified for employees, and costs minimized, through a standard default investment as well as electronic information and fund transfers. Workplace retirement savings arrangements made accessible to most workers also could be used as a platform to provide and promote retirement distributions annuitized over the worker's lifetime.

## Proposal

Employers in business for at least two years that have 10 or more employees would be required to offer an automatic IRA option to employees on a payroll-deduction basis, under which regular payroll-deduction contributions would be made to an IRA. If the employer sponsored a qualified retirement plan or SIMPLE for its employees, it would not be required to provide an automatic IRA option for any employee. Thus, for example, a qualified plan sponsor would not have to offer automatic IRAs to employees it excludes from qualified plan eligibility because they are collectively bargained, under age 18, nonresident aliens, or have not completed the plan's eligibility waiting period. However, if the qualified plan excluded from eligibility a portion of the employer's work force or a class of employees such as all employees of a subsidiary or division, the employer would be required to offer the automatic IRA option to those excluded employees.

The employer offering automatic IRAs would give employees a standard notice and election form informing them of the automatic IRA option and allowing them to elect to participate or opt out. Any employee who did not provide a written participation election would be enrolled at a default rate of three percent of the employee's compensation. Employees could opt for a lower or higher contribution rate up to the IRA dollar limits. For most employees, the payroll deductions would be made by direct deposit similar to the direct deposit of employees' paychecks to their accounts at financial institutions.

Payroll-deduction contributions from all participating employees could be transferred, at the employer's option, to a single private-sector IRA trustee or custodian designated by the employer. Alternatively, the employer, if it preferred, could allow each participating employee to designate the IRA provider for that employee's contributions or could designate that all contributions would be forwarded to a savings vehicle specified by statute or regulation.

Employers making payroll deduction IRAs available would not have to choose or arrange default investments. Instead, a low-cost, standard type of default investment and a handful of standard, low-cost investment alternatives would be prescribed by statute or regulation. In addition, this approach would involve no employer contributions, no employer compliance with qualified plan requirements, and no employer liability or responsibility for determining employee eligibility to make tax-favored IRA contributions or for opening IRAs for employees. A national web site would provide information and basic educational material regarding saving and investing for retirement, including IRA eligibility, but, as under current law, individuals (not employers) would bear ultimate responsibility for determining their IRA eligibility.

Employers could claim a temporary tax credit for making automatic payroll-deposit IRAs available to employees. The amount of the credit would be $25 per enrolled employee up to $250 each year for two years. The credit would be available both to employers required to offer automatic IRAs and employers not required to do so (for example, because they have fewer than ten employees).

Contributions by employees to automatic IRAs would qualify for the saver's credit (to the extent the contributor and the contributions otherwise qualified), and the proposed expanded saver's credit would be deposited to the IRA to which the eligible individual contributed.

The proposal would become effective January 1, 2012.

# PROVIDE THE AMERICAN OPPORTUNITY TAX CREDIT

## Current Law

Prior to ARRA an individual taxpayer could claim a nonrefundable Hope Scholarship credit for 100 percent of the first $1,200 and 50-percent of the next $1,200 in qualified tuition and related expenses (for a maximum credit of $1,800) per student. The Hope Scholarship credit was limited to the first two years of postsecondary education.

Alternatively, a taxpayer could claim a nonrefundable Lifetime Learning Credit (LLC) for 20 percent of up to $10,000 in qualified tuition and related expenses (for a maximum credit of $2,000) per taxpayer. Both the Hope Scholarship credit and LLC were phased out in 2009 between $50,000 and $60,000 of adjusted gross income ($100,000 and $120,000 if married filing jointly). In addition, through 2009, a taxpayer could claim an above-the-line deduction for qualified tuition and related expenses. The maximum amount of the deduction was $4,000.

ARRA created the American Opportunity Tax Credit (AOTC) to replace the Hope Scholarship Credit for taxable years 2009 and 2010. The new tax credit is partially refundable, has a higher maximum credit amount, is available for the first four years of postsecondary education, and has higher phase-out limits.

The AOTC equals 100 percent of the first $2,000 plus 25 percent of the next $2,000 of qualified tuition and related expenses (for a maximum credit of $2,500). Under ARRA, the definition of related expenses for both the LLC and the AOTC was expanded to include course materials. Forty percent of the otherwise allowable AOTC is refundable (for a maximum refundable credit of $1,000). The credit is available for the first four years of postsecondary education. The credit phases out for taxpayers with adjusted gross income between $80,000 and $90,000 ($160,000 and $180,000 if married filing jointly).

All other aspects of the Hope Scholarship credit are retained under the AOTC. These include the requirement that AOTC recipients be enrolled at least half-time.

## Reasons for Change

The AOTC makes college more affordable for millions of middle-income families and for the first time makes college tax incentives partially refundable. If college is not made more affordable, our nation runs the risk of losing a whole generation of potential and productivity.

Making the AOTC partially refundable increases the likelihood that low-income families will send their children to college. Under prior law, low-income families (those without sufficient tax liability) could not benefit from the Hope Scholarship credit because it was not refundable. Under the proposal, low-income families could benefit from both Federal Pell Grants and the refundable portion of the AOTC. In combination, these grants and credits would cover all tuition and fees at an average 2-year public college and about half of tuition and fees at an average 4-year public college.

Moreover, the new credit applies to the first four years of college, instead of only the first two years of college, increasing the likelihood that students will stay in school and attain their degrees. More years of schooling translates into higher future incomes for students and a more educated work force for the country.

Finally, the higher phase-out thresholds under the AOTC give targeted tax relief to an even greater number of middle-income families facing the high costs of college.

## Proposal

The proposal would make the AOTC a permanent replacement for the Hope Scholarship credit. To preserve the value of the AOTC, the proposal would index the $2,000 tuition and expense amounts, as well as the phase-out thresholds, for inflation.

This proposal would be effective for taxable years beginning after December 31, 2010.

# TAX CUTS FOR BUSINESS

## ELIMINATE CAPITAL GAINS TAXATION ON INVESTMENTS IN SMALL BUSINESS STOCK

### Current Law

Taxpayers other than corporations may exclude 50-percent (60 percent for certain empowerment zone businesses) of the gain from the sale of certain small business stock acquired at original issue and held for at least five years. Under ARRA the exclusion is increased to 75 percent for stock acquired in 2009 (after February 17, 2009) and in 2010. The taxable portion of the gain is taxed at a maximum rate of 28 percent. Under current law, 7 percent of the excluded gain is a tax preference subject to the alternative minimum tax (AMT). The AMT preference is scheduled to increase to 28 percent of the excluded gain on eligible stock acquired after December 31, 2000 and to 42 percent of the excluded gain on stock acquired on or before that date.

The amount of gain eligible for the exclusion by a taxpayer with respect to any corporation during any year is the greater of (1) ten times the taxpayer's basis in stock issued by the corporation and disposed of during the year, or (2) $10 million reduced by gain excluded in prior years on dispositions of the corporation's stock. To qualify as a small business, the corporation, when the stock is issued, may not have gross assets exceeding $50 million (including the proceeds of the newly issued stock) and may not be an S corporation.

The corporation also must meet certain active trade or business requirements. For example, the corporation must be engaged in a trade or business other than: one involving the performance of services in the fields of health, law, engineering, architecture, accounting, actuarial science, performing arts, consulting, athletics, financial services, brokerage services or any other trade or business where the principal asset of the trade or business is the reputation or skill of one or more employees; a banking, insurance, financing, leasing, investing or similar business; a farming business; a business involving production or extraction of items subject to depletion; or a hotel, motel, restaurant or similar business. There are limits on the amount of real property that may be held by a qualified small business, and ownership of, dealing in, or renting real property is not treated as an active trade or business.

### Reasons for Change

Because the taxable portion of gain from the sale of qualified small business stock is subject to tax at a maximum of 28 percent and a percentage of the excluded gain is a preference under the AMT, the current 50-percent provision provides little benefit. Increasing the exclusion would encourage and reward new investment in qualified small business stock.

### Proposal

Under the proposal the percentage exclusion for qualified small business stock sold by an individual or other non-corporate taxpayer would be increased to 100 percent and the AMT preference item for gain excluded under this provision would be eliminated. The stock would have to be held for at least five years and other provisions applying to the section 1202 exclusion would also apply. The proposal would include additional documentation requirements to assure compliance with the statute.

The proposal would be effective for qualified small business stock issued after February 17, 2009.

# MAKE THE RESEARCH & EXPERIMENTATION (R&E) TAX CREDIT PERMANENT

## Current Law

The research and experimentation (R&E) tax credit is 20 percent of qualified research expenses above a base amount. The base amount is the product of the taxpayer's "fixed base percentage" and the average of the taxpayer's gross receipts for the four preceding years. The taxpayer's fixed base percentage generally is the ratio of its research expenses to gross receipts for the 1984-88 period. The base amount cannot be less than 50-percent of the taxpayer's qualified research expenses for the taxable year. Taxpayers can elect the alternative simplified research credit (ASC), which is equal to 14 percent of qualified research expenses that exceed 50-percent of the average qualified research expenses for the three preceding taxable years. Under the ASC, the rate is reduced to 6 percent if a taxpayer has no qualified research expenses in any one of the three preceding taxable years. An election to use the ASC applies to all succeeding taxable years unless revoked with the consent of the Secretary.

The R&E tax credit also provides a credit for 20 percent of basic research payments in excess of a base amount and payments to an energy research consortium for energy research. The credit for energy research applies to all qualified expenditures, not solely those in excess of a base amount.

The R&E credit is scheduled to expire on December 31, 2009.

## Reasons for Change

The R&E tax credit encourages technological developments that are an important component of economic growth. However, uncertainty about the future availability of the R&E tax credit diminishes the incentive effect of the credit because it is difficult for taxpayers to factor the credit into decisions to invest in research projects that will not be initiated and completed prior to the credit's expiration. To improve the credit's effectiveness, the R&E tax credit should be made permanent.

## Proposal

The proposal would make the R&E credit permanent.

## EXPAND NET OPERATING LOSS CARRYBACK

### Current Law

A net operating loss (NOL) generally is the amount by which a taxpayer's business deductions exceed its gross income. For taxpayers other than certain eligible small businesses, an NOL may be carried back two years and carried forward 20 years to offset taxable income in such years. NOLs offset taxable income in the order of the taxable years to which the NOL may be carried. The AMT rules provide that a taxpayer's NOL deduction cannot reduce the taxpayer's alternative minimum taxable income (AMTI) by more than 90 percent of the AMTI.

Different rules apply with respect to NOLs arising in certain circumstances. A three-year carryback applies with respect to: (1) losses arising from casualty or theft losses of individuals, and (2) losses attributable to Presidentially declared disasters for taxpayers engaged in a farming business or a small business. A five-year carryback applies to: (1) farming losses (regardless of whether the loss was incurred in a Presidentially declared disaster area); (2) certain losses related to Hurricane Katrina, Gulf Opportunity Zone, and Midwestern Disaster Area; and (3) qualified disaster losses. Special rules also apply to real estate investment trusts (no carryback), specified liability losses (10-year carryback), and excess interest losses (no carryback to any year preceding a corporate equity reduction transaction). Additionally, a special rule applies to certain electric utility companies. In the case of a life insurance company, present law allows a deduction for the taxable year for operations loss carryovers and carrybacks in lieu of the deduction for NOLs allowed to other corporations. A life insurance company is permitted to treat a loss from operations for any taxable year as an operations loss carryback to each of the three taxable years preceding the loss year and an operations loss carryover to each of the 15 taxable years following the loss year. Special rules apply to new life insurance companies.

Most recently, the ARRA extended the carryback period for applicable 2008 NOLs to up to five years by certain eligible small businesses whose average annual gross receipts do not exceed $15,000,000.

### Reasons for Change

The NOL carryback and carryover rules are designed to allow taxpayers to smooth out swings in business income (and Federal income taxes thereon) that result from business cycle fluctuations. The recent economic conditions have resulted in many taxpayers incurring significant financial losses. A temporary extension of the NOL carryback period provides taxpayers in all sectors of the economy that experience such losses with the ability to obtain refunds of income taxes paid in prior years. These refunds can be used to fund capital investment or other operating expenses.

### Proposal

The Administration looks forward to working with the Congress to make a lengthened NOL carryback period available to more taxpayers.

# MODIFY FEDERAL AVIATION ADMINISTRATION FINANCING

## Current Law

The Airport and Airway Trust Fund is supported by taxes on air passenger transportation, domestic air freight transportation, and aviation fuel. The tax on domestic air passenger transportation is 7.5 percent of the amount paid for the transportation plus a segment fee of $3.60 per segment. The tax on international air transportation is $16.10 on each international arrival or departure. Both the segment fee and the international arrival and departure fee are adjusted annually for inflation. The tax on domestic air freight transportation is 6.25 percent of the amount paid for the transportation. The tax on aviation fuel, to the extent dedicated to the Airport and Airway Trust Fund, is 4.3 cents per gallon for kerosene used in commercial aviation, 21.8 cents per gallon for kerosene used in noncommercial (general) aviation, and 19.3 cents per gallon for aviation gasoline. The tax is generally imposed when the fuel is removed from a terminal.

The taxes that support the Airport and Airway Trust Fund expire on September 30, 2009. The taxes on air transportation do not apply to amounts paid after September 30, 2009. The taxes on aviation fuel do not apply to fuel removed from a terminal after September 30, 2009. The authority to make expenditures from the Trust Fund for airport and airway programs also expires on October 30, 2009.

## Reasons for Change

The Federal Aviation Administration's (FAA's) financing system should be more cost based. The current excise tax system, to the extent based on taxes on the amount paid for air transportation, does not provide a direct relationship between the taxes paid by users and the air traffic control services provided by the FAA. The Administration believes that the FAA should move toward a model whereby FAA's funding is related to its costs, the financing burden is distributed more equitably, and funds are used to pay directly for services the users need.

To provide for necessary Federal airport and airway expenditures until a cost-based system is developed, the aviation excise taxes and the expenditure authority from the Airport and Airway Trust Fund should be temporarily extended.

## Proposal

The taxes on air transportation and aviation fuel would be extended through September 30, 2011, at their current rates. Beginning October 1, 2011, the Budget assumes that the air traffic control system will be funded with direct charges levied on users of the system. The Budget reflects such a reform being in place starting in 2011, with a user charge collecting $9.6 billion in that year and with aviation excise taxes being commensurately reduced. Expenditure authority from the Airport and Airway Trust Fund would be extended through September 30, 2019.

# CONTINUE CERTAIN EXPIRING PROVISIONS THROUGH CALENDAR YEAR 2010

## Current Law

The existing tax code includes a number of provisions that are scheduled to expire before December 31, 2010. These provisions include the optional deduction for State and local general sales taxes, Subpart F "active financing" and "look-through" exceptions, the exclusion from unrelated business income of certain payments to controlling exempt organizations, the new markets tax credit, the modified recovery period for qualified leasehold improvements and qualified restaurant property, incentives for empowerment and community renewal zones, credits for biodiesel and renewable diesel fuels, and several trade agreements, including the Generalized System of Preferences and the Caribbean Basin Initiative.

## Reasons for Change.

In the past, these expiring provisions have been routinely extended. Extending them before they expire helps to provides certainty to taxpayers.

## Proposal

This proposal would extend these provisions through December 31, 2010.

# OTHER REVENUE CHANGES AND LOOPHOLE CLOSERS

## REINSTATE SUPERFUND EXCISE TAXES

### Current Law

The following Superfund excise taxes were imposed before January 1, 1996:

(1) An excise tax on domestic crude oil and on imported petroleum products at a rate of 9.7 cents per barrel;

(2) An excise tax on listed hazardous chemicals at a rate that varied from $0.22 to $4.87 per ton; and

(3) An excise tax on imported substances that use as materials in their manufacture or production one or more of the hazardous chemicals subject to the excise tax described in (2) above.

Amounts equivalent to the revenues from these taxes were dedicated to the Hazardous Substance Superfund Trust Fund (the Superfund Trust Fund). Amounts in the Superfund Trust Fund are available for expenditures incurred in connection with releases or threats of releases of hazardous substances into the environment under specified provisions of the Comprehensive Environmental Response, Compensation, and Liability Act of 1980 (as amended).

### Reasons for Change

The Superfund excise taxes should be reinstated because of the continuing need for funds to remedy damages caused by releases of hazardous substances.

### Proposal

The three Superfund excise taxes would be reinstated for periods after December 31, 2010.

# REINSTATE SUPERFUND ENVIRONMENTAL INCOME TAX

## Current Law

For taxable years beginning before January 1, 1996, a corporate environmental income tax was imposed at a rate of 0.12 percent on the amount by which the modified alternative minimum taxable income of a corporation exceeded $2 million. Modified alternative minimum taxable income was defined as a corporation's alternative minimum taxable income, determined without regard to the alternative minimum tax net operating loss deduction and the deduction for the corporate environmental income tax.

The tax was dedicated to the Hazardous Substance Superfund Trust Fund (the Superfund Trust Fund). Amounts in the Superfund Trust Fund are available for expenditures incurred in connection with releases or threats of releases of hazardous substances into the environment under specified provisions of the Comprehensive Environmental Response, Compensation, and Liability Act of 1980 (as amended).

## Reasons for Change

The corporate environmental income tax should be reinstated because of the continuing need for funds to remedy damages caused by releases of hazardous substances.

## Proposal

The corporate environmental income tax would be reinstated for taxable years beginning after December 31, 2010.

# TAX CARRIED (PROFIT) INTERESTS AS ORDINARY INCOME

## Current Law

A partnership is not subject to federal income tax. Instead, income and loss of the partnership retains its character and flows through to its partners, who must include such items on their tax returns. Generally, certain partners receive partnership interests in exchange for contributions of cash and/or property, while certain partners (not necessarily other partners) receive partnership interests, typically interests in future profits ("profits interests") in exchange for services. Accordingly, if and to the extent a partnership recognizes long-term capital gain, the partners, including partners who provide services, will reflect their shares of such gain on their tax returns as long-term capital gain. If the partner is an individual, such gain would be taxed at the reduced rates for long-term capital gains. Gain recognized on the sale of a partnership interest, whether it was received in exchange for property, cash or services, is generally treated as capital gain.

Under current law, income attributable to a profits interest of a general partner is generally subject to self-employment tax, except to the extent the partnership generates types of income that are excluded from self employment taxes, e.g., capital gains, certain interest and dividends.

## Reason for Change

Although profits interests are structured as partnership interests, the income allocable to such interests is received in connection with the performance of services. A service provider's share of the income of a partnership attributable to a carried interest should be taxed as ordinary income and subject to self-employment tax because such income is derived from the performance of services. By allowing service partners to receive capital gains treatment on labor income without limit, the current system creates an unfair and inefficient tax preference. The recent explosion of activity among large private equity firms has increased the breadth and cost of this tax preference, with some of the highest-income Americans benefiting from the preferential treatment.

## Proposal

A partner's share of income on a "services partnership interest" (SPI) would be subject to tax as ordinary income, regardless of the character of the income at the partnership level. Accordingly, such income would not be eligible for the reduced rates that apply to long-term capital gains. In addition, the proposal would require the partner to pay self-employment taxes on such income. Gain recognized on the sale of an SPI would generally be taxed as ordinary income, not as capital gain.

An SPI is a carried interest held by a person who provides services to the partnership. To the extent that the partner who holds an SPI contributes "invested capital" and the partnership reasonably allocates its income and loss between such invested capital and the remaining interest, income attributable to the invested capital would not be recharacterized. Similarly, the portion of any gain recognized on the sale of an SPI that is attributable to the invested capital would be treated as capital gain. "Invested capital" is defined as money or other property contributed to the partnership. However, contributed capital that is attributable to the proceeds of any loan or other advance made or guaranteed by any partner or the partnership is not treated as "invested capital."

Also, any person who performs services for an entity and holds a "disqualified interest" in the entity is subject to ordinary income tax on any income or gain received with respect to the interest. A "disqualified interest" is defined as convertible or contingent debt, an option, or any derivative instrument with respect to the entity (but does not include a partnership interest or stock in certain taxable corporations). This is an anti-abuse rule designed to prevent the avoidance of the proposal through the use of compensatory arrangements other than partnership interests.

The proposal is not intended to adversely impact qualification of a real estate investment trust owning a carried interest in a real estate partnership.

The proposal would be effective for taxable years beginning after December 31, 2010.

# CODIFY "ECONOMIC SUBSTANCE" DOCTRINE

## Current Law

*Economic Substance Doctrine.* The common-law "economic substance" doctrine generally denies tax benefits from a transaction that does not meaningfully change a taxpayer's economic position, other than tax consequences, even if the transaction literally satisfies the requirements of the Internal Revenue Code. Although courts have applied the economic substance doctrine with increasing frequency, they have not applied it uniformly. Some courts require both (i) a meaningful change to the taxpayer's economic position (referred to as "objective" economic substance), and (ii) a substantial non-tax business purpose, while other courts require only one of the two factors to satisfy the economic substance doctrine. Still other courts consider objective economic substance and business purpose to be only two factors in a general investigation into whether a transaction has economic effects other than tax benefits.

*Accuracy-Related Penalties.* Current law contains an accuracy-related penalty that applies to an underpayment of tax attributable to a substantial understatement of income tax. The penalty equals 20 percent of the tax underpayment. Except in the case of tax shelters, the penalty may be reduced if (i) the taxpayer's treatment is supported by substantial authority or (ii) the relevant facts were adequately disclosed, and there is a reasonable basis for the item's tax treatment. A separate 20-percent penalty applies to an understatement of income tax attributable to a "listed transaction" or a "reportable transaction" with a significant purpose of tax avoidance or evasion. The penalty rate is increased to 30 percent if the taxpayer has not disclosed the transaction as required by law. Either penalty may be set aside or reduced if the taxpayer can demonstrate that there was "reasonable cause" for the taxpayer's position and that the taxpayer acted in good faith.

*Denial of Interest Deduction.* Current law denies any deduction for interest paid with respect to a reportable transaction understatement where the relevant facts were not adequately disclosed.

## Reason for Change

Clarifying the economic substance doctrine and increasing the penalty for transactions that lack economic substance will further deter transactions designed solely to obtain tax benefits.

## Proposal

*Clarification of Economic Substance Doctrine.* The proposal would clarify that a transaction satisfies the economic substance doctrine only if (i) it changes in a meaningful way (apart from federal tax effects) the taxpayer's economic position, and (ii) the taxpayer has a substantial purpose (other than a federal tax purpose) for entering into the transaction. The proposal would also clarify that a transaction will not be treated as having economic substance solely by reason of a profit potential unless the present value of the reasonably expected pre-tax profit is substantial in relation to the present value of the net federal tax benefits arising from the transaction. The proposal would allow the Treasury Department to publish regulations to carry out the purposes of the proposal.

*New Understatement Penalty.* The proposal would impose a 30-percent penalty on an understatement of tax attributable to a transaction that lacks economic substance, reduced to 20 percent if there were adequate disclosure of the relevant facts in the taxpayer's return. The proposed penalty would be imposed with regard to an understatement due to a transaction's lack of economic substance in lieu of other accuracy-related penalties that might be levied with respect to the tax understatement, although any understatement arising from a lack of economic substance would be taken into account in determining whether there is a substantial understatement of income tax under current law.

The IRS could assert and abate the new economic substance penalty. The IRS could assert the penalty even if there has not been a court determination that the economic substance doctrine was relevant. Any abatement of the economic substance penalty would have to be proportionate to the abatement of the underlying tax liability.

*Denial of Interest Deduction.* The proposal would deny any deduction for interest attributable to an understatement of tax arising from the application of the economic substance doctrine.

The proposal would apply to transactions entered into after the date of enactment. The denial of interest deduction component would be effective for taxable years ending after the date of enactment with respect to transactions entered into after such date.

## REPEAL THE LAST-IN, FIRST-OUT (LIFO) METHOD OF ACCOUNTING FOR INVENTORIES

### Current Law

The Internal Revenue Code (Code) permits a taxpayer with inventories to determine the value of its inventory and its cost of goods sold using a number of different methods. The most prevalent method is the first-in, first-out (FIFO) method, which matches current sales with the costs of the earliest acquired (or manufactured) inventory items. As an alternative, a taxpayer may elect to use the last-in, first-out (LIFO) method, which treats the most recently acquired (or manufactured) goods as having been sold during the year. The LIFO method can provide a tax benefit for a taxpayer facing rising inventory costs, since the cost of goods sold under this method is based on more recent, higher inventory values, resulting in lower taxable income. If inventory levels fall during the year, however, a LIFO taxpayer must include lower-cost LIFO inventory values (reflecting one or more prior-year inventory accumulations) in the cost of goods sold, and its taxable income will be correspondingly higher. To be eligible to elect LIFO for tax purposes, a taxpayer must use LIFO for financial accounting purposes.

### Reasons for Change

The repeal of LIFO would eliminate a tax deferral opportunity that is available to taxpayers that possess inventories whose costs increase over time. In addition, LIFO repeal would simplify the Code by removing a complex and burdensome accounting method that has been the source of controversy between taxpayers and the IRS.

International Financial Reporting Standards do not permit the use of the LIFO method, and their adoption by the Security and Exchange Commission would cause violations of the current LIFO book/tax conformity requirement. Repealing LIFO removes this possible impediment to the implementation of these standards in the United States.

### Proposal

The proposal would not allow the use of the LIFO inventory accounting method for Federal income tax purposes. Taxpayers that currently use the LIFO method would be required to write up their beginning LIFO inventory to its FIFO value in the first taxable year beginning after December 31, 2011. However, this one-time increase in gross income would be taken into account ratably over the first taxable year and the following seven taxable years.

**Reform U.S. International Tax System**

## REFORM BUSINESS ENTITY CLASSIFICATION RULES FOR FOREIGN ENTITIES

### Current Law

Under current Treasury regulations, an eligible business entity can elect its classification for federal tax purposes. An eligible business entity with a single owner may elect to be treated as a corporation or as an entity disregarded as an entity separate from its owner (a "disregarded entity"). An eligible business entity with at least two owners may elect to be treated as a partnership or as a corporation. Certain foreign entities are always treated as corporations for federal tax purposes (so called "per se corporations").

### Reasons for Change

As applied to foreign eligible entities, the entity classification rules may result in the unintended avoidance of current U.S. tax, particularly if a foreign eligible entity elects to be treated as a disregarded entity. In certain cases, locating a foreign disregarded entity under a centralized holding company (or partnership) may permit the migration of earnings to low-taxed jurisdictions without a current income inclusion of the amount of such earnings to a U.S. taxpayer under the subpart F provisions of the Code.

### Proposal

Under the proposal, a foreign eligible entity may be treated as a disregarded entity only if the single owner of the foreign eligible entity is created or organized in, or under the law of, the foreign country in, or under the law of, which the foreign eligible entity is created or organized. Therefore, a foreign eligible entity with a single owner that is organized or created in a country other than that of its single owner would be treated as a corporation for federal tax purposes. Except in cases of U.S. tax avoidance, the proposal would generally not apply to a first-tier foreign eligible entity wholly owned by a United States person. The tax treatment of the conversion to a corporation of a foreign eligible entity treated as a disregarded entity would be consistent with current Treasury regulations and relevant tax principles.

The proposal would be effective for taxable years beginning after December 31, 2010.

## DEFER DEDUCTION OF EXPENSES, EXCEPT R&E EXPENSES, RELATED TO DEFERRED INCOME

### Current Law

Taxpayers generally may deduct ordinary and necessary expenses paid or incurred in carrying on any trade or business. The Internal Revenue Code and the regulations thereunder contain detailed rules regarding allocation and apportionment of expenses for computing taxable income from sources within and without the United States.

### Reasons for Change

Under current law, a U.S. person that incurs expenses properly allocable and apportioned to foreign-source income may deduct those expenses even if the expenses exceed the taxpayer's gross foreign-source income or if the taxpayer earns no foreign-source income. For example, a U.S. person that incurs debt to acquire stock of a foreign corporation is generally permitted to deduct currently the interest expense from the acquisition indebtedness even if no income is derived currently from such stock. The U.S. person is also permitted to deduct currently other expenses properly allocated or apportioned to the stock of the foreign corporation. Current law includes provisions that may require a U.S. person to recapture as U.S.-source income the amount by which foreign-source expenses exceed foreign-source income for a taxable year. However, if in a taxable year the U.S. person earns sufficient foreign-source income of the same statutory grouping in which the stock of the foreign corporation is classified, the interest and other expenses properly allocated and apportioned to the stock of the foreign corporation may not be subject to recapture in a subsequent taxable year. This ability to deduct expenses from overseas investments while deferring U.S. tax on the income from the investment may cause U.S. businesses to shift their investments and jobs overseas, harming our domestic economy.

### Proposal

The proposal would defer a deduction for expenses (other than research and experimentation expenditures) of a U.S. person that are properly allocated and apportioned to foreign-source income to the extent the foreign-source income associated with the expenses is not currently subject to U.S. tax. The amount of expenses properly allocated and apportioned to foreign-source income generally would be determined under current Treasury regulations. The amount of deferred expenses for a particular year would be carried forward to subsequent years and combined with the foreign-source expenses of the U.S. person for such year before determining the impact of the proposal in such year.

The proposal would be effective for taxable years beginning after December 31, 2010.

## REFORM FOREIGN TAX CREDIT: DETERMINE THE FOREIGN TAX CREDIT ON A POOLING BASIS

### Current Law

Section 901 provides that, subject to certain limitations, a taxpayer may choose to claim a credit against its U.S. income tax liability for income, war profits, and excess profits taxes paid or accrued during the taxable year to any foreign country or any possession of the United States. Under section 902, a domestic corporation is deemed to have paid the foreign taxes paid by certain foreign subsidiaries from which it receives a dividend (the deemed paid foreign tax credit). The foreign tax credit is limited to an amount equal to the pre-credit U.S. tax on the taxpayer's foreign-source income. This foreign tax credit limitation is applied separately to foreign-source income in each of the separate categories described in section 904(d), i.e., the passive category and general category.

### Reasons for Change

The purpose of the foreign tax credit is to mitigate the potential for double taxation when U.S. taxpayers are subject to foreign taxes on their foreign-source income. The reduction to two foreign tax credit limitation categories for passive category income and general category income under the American Jobs Creation Act of 2004 enhanced U.S. taxpayers' ability through "cross-crediting" to reduce the residual U.S. tax on foreign-source income.

### Proposal

Under the proposal, a U.S. taxpayer would determine its deemed paid foreign tax credit on a consolidated basis by determining the aggregate foreign taxes and earnings and profits of all of the foreign subsidiaries with respect to which the U.S. taxpayer can claim a deemed paid foreign tax credit (including lower tier subsidiaries described section 902(b)). The deemed paid foreign tax credit for a taxable year would be determined based on the amount of the consolidated earnings and profits of the foreign subsidiaries repatriated to the U.S. taxpayer in that taxable year.

The proposal would be effective for taxable years beginning after December 31, 2010.

## REFORM FOREIGN TAX CREDIT: PREVENT SPLITTING OF FOREIGN INCOME AND FOREIGN TAXES

### Current Law

Section 901 provides that, subject to certain limitations, a taxpayer may choose to claim a credit against its U.S. income tax liability for income, war profits, and excess profits taxes paid or accrued during the taxable year to any foreign country or any possession of the United States. Under current law, the person considered to have paid the foreign tax is the person on whom foreign law imposes legal liability for such tax.

### Reasons for Change

Current law permits inappropriate separation of creditable foreign taxes from the associated foreign income in certain cases such as those involving hybrid arrangements.

### Proposal

The proposal would adopt a matching rule to prevent the separation of creditable foreign taxes from the associated foreign income.

The proposal would be effective for taxable years beginning after December 31, 2010.

# LIMIT SHIFTING OF INCOME THROUGH INTANGIBLE PROPERTY TRANSFERS

## Current Law

Section 482 permits the Commissioner to distribute, apportion, or allocate gross income, deductions, credits, and other allowances between or among two or more organizations, trades, or businesses under common ownership or control whenever "necessary in order to prevent evasion of taxes or clearly to reflect the income of any of such organizations, trades, or businesses." Section 482 also provides that in the case of any transfer (or license) of intangible property (as defined in section 936(h)(3)(B)), the income with respect to such transfer or license must be commensurate with the income attributable to the intangible property. Further, under section 367(d), if a U.S. person transfers intangible property (as defined in section 936(h)(3)(B)) to a foreign corporation in certain nonrecognition transactions, the U.S. person is treated as selling the intangible property for a series of payments contingent on the productivity, use, or disposition of the property that are commensurate with the transferee's income from the property. The payments generally continue annually over the useful life of the property.

## Reasons for Change

Controversy often arises concerning the value of intangible property transferred between related persons. Further, the scope of the intangible property subject to sections 482 and 367(d) is not entirely clear or consistent. This lack of clarity and consistency may result in the inappropriate avoidance of U.S. tax and misuse of the rules applicable to transfers of intangible property to foreign persons.

## Proposal

To prevent inappropriate shifting of income outside the United States, the proposal would clarify the definition of intangible property for purposes of sections 367(d) and 482 to include workforce in place, goodwill and going concern value. The proposal would also clarify that in a transfer of multiple intangible properties, the Commissioner may value the intangible properties on an aggregate basis where that achieves a more reliable result. The proposal would also clarify that intangible property must be valued at its highest and best use, as it would change hands between a willing buyer and a willing seller, neither being under any compulsion to buy or to sell and both having reasonable knowledge of relevant facts.

The proposal would be effective for taxable years beginning after December 31, 2010.

# LIMIT EARNINGS STRIPPING BY EXPATRIATED ENTITIES

## Current Law

Section 163(j) applies to limit the deductibility of certain interest paid by a corporation to related persons. The limitation applies to a corporation that fails a debt-to-equity safe harbor (greater than 1.5 to 1) and that has net interest expense in excess of 50 percent of adjusted taxable income (computed by adding back net interest expense, depreciation, amortization and depletion, and any net operating loss deduction). Disallowed interest expense may be carried forward indefinitely for deduction in a subsequent year. In addition, the corporations's excess limitation for a tax year (i.e., the amount by which 50 percent of adjusted taxable income exceeds net interest expense) may be carried forward to the three subsequent tax years.

Section 7874 provides special rules for expatriated entities and the acquiring foreign corporations. The rules apply to certain defined transactions in which a U.S. parent company (the expatriated entity) is essentially replaced with a foreign parent (the surrogate foreign corporation). The tax treatment of an expatriated entity and a surrogate foreign corporation varies depending on the extent of continuity of shareholder ownership following the transaction. The surrogate foreign corporation is treated as a domestic corporation for all purposes of the Code if shareholder ownership continuity is at least 80 percent (by vote or value). If shareholder ownership continuity is at least 60 percent, but less than 80 percent, the surrogate foreign corporation is treated as a foreign corporation but any applicable corporate-level income or gain required to be recognized by the expatriated entity generally cannot be offset by tax attributes. Section 7874 generally applies to transactions occurring on or after March 4, 2003.

## Reasons for Change

Under current law, opportunities are available to reduce inappropriately the U.S. tax on income earned from U.S. operations through the use of foreign related-party debt. In its recent study of earnings stripping, the Treasury Department found strong evidence of the use of such techniques by expatriated entities. Consequently, amending the rules of section 163(j) for expatriated entities is necessary to prevent these inappropriate income-reduction opportunities. Because the study did not find conclusive evidence of earnings stripping by foreign-controlled domestic corporations that have not expatriated, additional information is needed to determine whether changes to section 163(j) should be made with respect to those companies. The new Form 8926, Disqualified Corporate Interest Expense Disallowed Under Section 163(j) and Related Information, should assist in obtaining this information.

## Proposal

The proposal would revise section 163(j) to tighten the limitation on the deductibility of interest paid by an expatriated entity to related persons. The current law debt-to-equity safe harbor would be eliminated. The 50 percent adjusted taxable income threshold for the limitation would be reduced to 25 percent of adjusted taxable income with respect to disqualified interest other than interest paid to unrelated parties on debt that is subject to a related-party guarantee ("guaranteed debt"). The 50 percent adjusted taxable income threshold would generally contine to apply to interest on guaranteed debt. The carryforward for disallowed interest would be limited to ten years and the carryforward of excess limitation would be eliminated.

An expatriated entity would be defined by applying the rules of section 7874 and the regulations thereunder as if section 7874 were applicable for taxable years beginning after July 10, 1989. This special rule would not apply, however, if the surrogate foreign corporation is treated as a domestic corporation under section 7874.

The proposal would be effective for taxable years beginning after December 31, 2010.

## PREVENT REPATRIATION OF EARNINGS IN CERTAIN CROSS-BORDER REORGANIZATIONS

### Current Law

Under section 356(a)(1), if as part of a reorganization transaction an exchanging shareholder receives in exchange for its stock of the target corporation both stock and property that cannot be received without the recognition of gain (so-called "boot"), the exchanging shareholder is required to recognize gain equal to the lesser of the gain realized in the exchange or the amount of boot received (commonly referred to as the "boot within gain" limitation). Further, under section 356(a)(2), if the exchange has the effect of the distribution of a dividend, then all or part of the gain recognized by the exchanging shareholder is treated as a dividend to the extent of the shareholder's ratable share of the corporation's earnings and profits. The remainder of the gain (if any) is treated as gain from the exchange of property.

### Reasons for Change

In cross-border reorganizations, the boot-within-gain limitation of current law can permit U.S. shareholders to repatriate previously-untaxed earnings and profits of foreign subsidiaries with minimal U.S. tax consequences. For example, if the exchanging shareholder's stock in the target corporation has little or no built-in gain at the time of the exchange, the shareholder will recognize minimal gain even if the exchange has the effect of the distribution of a dividend and/or a significant amount (or all) of the consideration received in the exchange is boot. This result applies even if the corporation has previously untaxed earnings and profits equal to or greater than the boot. This result is inconsistent with the principle that previously untaxed earnings and profits of a foreign subsidiary should be subject to U.S. tax upon repatriation.

### Proposal

The proposal would repeal the boot-within-gain limitation of current law in the case of any reorganization in which the acquiring corporation is foreign and the shareholder's exchange has the effect of the distribution of a dividend, as determined under section 356(a)(2).

The proposal would be effective for taxable years beginning after December 31, 2010.

## REPEAL 80/20 COMPANY RULES

### Current Law

Dividends and interest paid by a domestic corporation are generally U.S.-source income to the recipient and are generally subject to gross basis withholding tax if paid to a foreign person. A limited exception to these general rules applies with respect to a domestic corporation (a so-called "80/20" company) if at least 80 percent of the corporation's gross income during a three-year testing period is foreign-source and attributable to the active conduct of a foreign trade or business. Look-through rules apply to determine the character of certain income of the 80/20 company for this purpose.

### Reasons for Change

The 80/20 company provisions can be manipulated and should be repealed.

### Proposal

The proposal would repeal the 80/20 company provisions under current law.

The proposal would be effective for taxable years beginning after December 31, 2010.

# PREVENT THE AVOIDANCE OF DIVIDEND WITHHOLDING TAXES

## Current Law

A withholding agent generally must withhold a tax of 30 percent from the gross amount of all U.S.-source fixed or determinable annual or periodical (FDAP) income, profits, or gains of a nonresident alien individual, foreign corporation, or foreign partnership. In general, dividends paid with respect to the stock of a domestic corporation are U.S.-source dividends. Thus, foreign investors holding stock in domestic corporations are generally subject to 30 percent tax on dividends paid with respect to that stock. This rate may be reduced where the dividends are paid to a resident of a jurisdiction with which the United States has entered into a tax treaty.

The source of income from notional principal contracts is generally determined based on the residence of the investor. As a result, substitute dividend payments made to a foreign investor with respect to an equity swap referencing U.S. equities are treated as foreign-source and are therefore not subject to U.S. withholding tax.

## Reason for Change

Foreign portfolio investors seeking to benefit from the appreciation in value and dividends paid with respect to the stock of a domestic corporation are not limited to holding stock in the corporation. Instead, such an investor can enter into an equity swap. The U.S. tax consequences of these two alternative investments differ significantly. By entering into equity swaps, foreign portfolio investors receive the economic benefit of dividends paid and appreciation in value with respect to U.S. stock without being subject to gross-basis withholding tax.

## Proposal

In order to address the avoidance of U.S. withholding tax through the use of securities lending transactions, the Treasury Department plans to revoke Notice 97-66 and issue guidance that eliminates the benefits of such transactions but minimizes over-withholding.

Further, income earned by foreign persons with respect to equity swaps that reference U.S. equities would be treated as U.S.-source to the extent that the income is attributable to (or calculated by reference to) dividends paid by a domestic corporation. An exception to this source rule would apply to swaps with all of the following characteristics:

- the terms of the equity swap do not require the foreign person to post more than 20 percent of the value of the underlying stock as collateral;
- the terms of the equity swap do not include any provision addressing the hedge position of the counterparty to the transaction;
- the underlying stock is publicly traded and the notional amount of the swap represents less than 5 percent of the total public float of that class of stock and less than 20 percent of the 30-day average daily trading volume;
- the foreign person does not sell the stock to the counterparty at the inception of the contract, or buy the stock from the counterparty at the termination of the contract;

- the prices of the equity that are used to measure the parties' entitlements or obligations are based on an objectively observable price; and
- the swap has a term of at least 90 days.

The Treasury Department would be given regulatory authority to provide additional exceptions to implement the purpose of the rule.

The proposal would be effective for payments made after December 31, 2010.

# MODIFY THE TAX RULES FOR DUAL CAPACITY TAXPAYERS

## Current Law

Section 901 provides that, subject to certain limitations, a taxpayer may choose to claim a credit against its U.S. income tax liability for income, war profits, and excess profits taxes paid or accrued during the taxable year to any foreign country or any possession of the United States. To be a creditable tax, a foreign levy must be substantially equivalent to an income tax under U.S. tax principles, regardless of the label attached to the levy under foreign law. Under current Treasury regulations, a foreign levy is a tax if it is a compulsory payment under the authority of a foreign government to levy taxes and is not compensation for a specific economic benefit provided by the foreign country. Taxpayers that are subject to a foreign levy and that also receive a specific economic benefit from the levying country (dual-capacity taxpayers) may not credit the portion of the foreign levy paid for the specific economic benefit. The current Treasury regulations provide that, if a foreign country has a generally imposed income tax, the dual-capacity taxpayer may treat as a creditable tax the portion of the levy that application of the generally imposed income tax would yield (provided that the levy otherwise constitutes an income tax or an in lieu of tax). The balance of the levy is treated as compensation for the specific economic benefit. If the foreign country does not generally impose an income tax, the portion of the payment that does not exceed the applicable federal tax rate applied to net income is treated as a creditable tax. A foreign tax is treated as generally imposed even if it applies only to persons who are not residents or nationals of that country.

There is no section 904 foreign tax credit separate category for foreign oil and gas income. However, under section 907, the amount of creditable foreign taxes imposed on foreign oil and gas income is limited in any year to the applicable U.S. tax on that income.

## Reasons for Change

The purpose of the foreign tax credit is to mitigate double taxation of income by the United States and a foreign country. When a payment is made to a foreign country in exchange for a specific economic benefit, there is no double taxation. Current law recognizes the distinction between creditable taxes and non-creditable payments for a specific economic benefit but fails to achieve the appropriate split between the two in a case where a foreign country imposes a levy on, for example, oil and gas income only, but has no generally imposed income tax.

## Proposal

In the case of a dual-capacity taxpayer, the proposal would treat a foreign levy that would otherwise qualify as an income tax or in lieu of tax as a creditable tax only if the foreign country generally imposes an income tax. An income tax would be considered generally imposed for this purpose only if the income tax applies to trade or business income from sources in that country, and only if the income tax has substantial application to non-dual-capacity taxpayers and to persons who are nationals or residents of that country. The proposal would replace the part of the regulatory safe harbor that applies when a foreign country does not generally impose an income tax. The proposal generally would retain the rule of present law where the foreign country does generally impose an income tax. The proposal also would convert the special foreign tax credit limitation rules of section 907 into a separate category within section 904 for foreign oil and gas income. The proposal would yield to U.S. treaty obligations that allow a credit for taxes paid or accrued on certain oil or gas income.

The proposal would be effective for taxable years beginning after December 31, 2010.

**Combat Under-Reporting of Income Through Use of Accounts and Entities in Offshore Jurisdictions**

The Administration is concerned about the use of offshore accounts and entities by certain U.S. and foreign persons to evade U.S. tax. To reduce such evasion, the Administration is proposing a series of measures to strengthen the information reporting and withholding systems that support U.S. taxation of income earned or held through offshore accounts or entities.

The qualified intermediary (QI) program is intended to bring foreign financial institutions more directly into the U.S. information reporting and withholding tax system, thereby helping to ensure that foreign persons are subject to the proper U.S. withholding tax. Strengthening the withholding and reporting rules under which QIs operate with respect to U.S. and foreign persons while creating incentives for more foreign financial institutions to become QIs will help to ensure that U.S. persons are properly paying tax in connection with foreign income and accounts and that proper withholding tax applies with respect to foreign persons.

## REQUIRE GREATER REPORTING BY QUALIFIED INTERMEDIARIES REGARDING U.S. ACCOUNT HOLDERS

### Current Law

A withholding agent generally must withhold tax at a rate of 30 percent from the gross amount of all U.S.-source fixed or determinable annual or periodical gains, profits, or income (FDAP income) of a nonresident alien individual or foreign entity. A payor is generally required to withhold tax at a rate of 28 percent on a reportable payment made to a U.S. non-exempt recipient if the payee fails to provide a taxpayer identification number or fails to certify, when required, that the payee is not subject to backup withholding, or the payor is notified by the IRS or a broker that the payee is subject to backup withholding.

Treasury regulations address certification, documentation, withholding, and reporting of payments to U.S. and foreign persons through foreign financial institutions. Foreign financial institutions may contract with the IRS to operate according to a set of withholding and reporting rules under the so-called "qualified intermediary" (QI) program. QIs agree to collect identifying documentation from their customers, file withholding tax returns and information returns, and submit to periodic audits performed by external auditors supervised by IRS examiners. QIs may furnish a withholding certificate to a withholding agent in lieu of transmitting to the withholding agent documentation for persons for whom the QI receives the payment and, in the case of U.S. non-exempt recipients, assumes primary Form 1099 reporting and backup withholding responsibility.

QIs need not assume primary Form 1099 reporting and backup withholding responsibility. If a QI nevertheless assumes primary Form 1099 reporting and backup withholding responsibility with respect to accounts held by U.S. persons, such reporting may be limited to certain income earned through those accounts. Further, a QI that assumes primary Form 1099 reporting and backup withholding responsibility with respect to U.S. persons is not required to assume that responsibility for all accounts. Moreover, in the case of financial institutions that are part of a controlled group, one member of the controlled group may contract to be a QI while other members of the controlled group do not, and thus accounts and clients may be divided between commonly-controlled QI and non-QI institutions.

## Reasons for Change

Strengthening the withholding and reporting rules under which QIs operate with respect to U.S. persons while creating incentives for the use of QIs would help to ensure that U.S. persons are properly paying tax on income earned through foreign accounts and that proper withholding tax applies with respect to foreign persons. In order to facilitate operation of this strengthened QI program, a list of QIs must be made publicly available.

## Proposal

Under the proposal, no foreign financial institution would qualify as a QI unless it identifies all of its account holders that are U.S. persons. A QI would be required to report all reportable payments (for this purpose, treating the QI as a U.S. payor) received on behalf of all U.S. account holders. Thus, a QI would file Form 1099s with respect to payments to those U.S. account holders as though the QI were a U.S. financial institution. The Treasury Department would be authorized to issue regulations to implement the purposes of this proposal, including authority to require that for any financial institution to be a QI, commonly-controlled foreign financial institutions must meet certain reporting obligations with respect to account holders or that a financial institution may be a QI only if all commonly-controlled financial institutions are also QIs, and including authority to provide that for any financial institution to be a QI it must collect information indicating the beneficial owners of foreign entity account holders and specifically report if a U.S. person is a beneficial owner. The proposal would also clarify that under section 6103 of the Code the IRS may publish the list of QIs.

The proposal would be effective beginning after December 31 of the year of enactment.

# REQUIRE WITHHOLDING ON PAYMENTS OF FDAP INCOME MADE THROUGH NONQUALIFIED INTERMEDIARIES

## Current Law

In general, payments of U.S.-source fixed or determinable annual or periodical gains, profits, or income (FDAP income) to nonresident alien individuals and foreign entities are subject to withholding tax at a rate of 30 percent. This 30-percent withholding tax may be reduced or eliminated pursuant to certain statutory provisions or pursuant to the terms of a tax treaty.

To determine whether the recipient of a payment is exempt from withholding tax or eligible for a reduced rate, withholding agents generally must rely on beneficial ownership documentation provided by the payee certifying that the payee is entitled to an exemption from withholding tax or a reduced rate of withholding tax under a Code provision or relevant tax treaty. In general, withholding agents are entitled to rely on the self-certification they receive absent actual knowledge or reason to know that the information provided is incorrect or unreliable. In the case of payments made through an intermediary, the intermediary generally provides to the withholding agent the appropriate documentation on behalf of the payment's beneficial owners.

## Reasons for Change

The Administration is concerned that some persons that are not entitled to an exemption from withholding tax or a reduced rate of withholding tax may attempt to avoid U.S. tax by arranging to receive payments through foreign intermediaries that are not qualified intermediaries (nonqualified intermediaries). The proposal would discourage U.S. and foreign persons from attempting to avoid U.S. tax or to obtain a lower rate of withholding tax by providing incorrect self-certification or otherwise relying on the lack of information reporting associated with using nonqualified intermediaries. The proposal would also encourage use of the strengthened qualified intermediary system, by requiring withholding of tax on payments made through nonqualified intermediaries.

## Proposal

Any withholding agent making a payment of FDAP income to a nonqualified intermediary would be required to treat the payment as made to an unknown foreign person (and therefore to withhold tax at a rate of 30 percent). The Treasury Department would receive regulatory authority to provide exceptions, including exceptions for payments collected by nonqualified intermediaries for foreign government, central bank, foreign pension fund, and foreign insurance company payees, and other similar investors, and for payments that the Treasury Department concludes present a low risk of tax evasion. The rules will be designed so as not to disrupt ordinary and customary market transactions. Foreign persons that are subject to over-withholding as a result of this proposal would be permitted to apply for a refund of any excess tax withheld.

The proposal would be effective for payments made after December 31 of the year of enactment.

# REQUIRE WITHHOLDING ON GROSS PROCEEDS PAID TO CERTAIN NONQUALIFIED INTERMEDIARIES

## Current Law

Brokers are generally required to withhold tax at a rate of 28 percent on certain reportable payments made to a U.S. non-exempt recipient if the payee fails to provide a taxpayer identification number or fails to certify that the payee is not subject to backup withholding, or the payor is notified by the IRS or a broker that the payee is subject to backup withholding. Reportable payments include the gross proceeds from certain transactions effected by brokers for their customers. A broker is exempt from reporting a payment (and thus backup withholding) where the broker can, prior to payment, associate the payment with documentation upon which it can rely to either treat the customer as a foreign beneficial owner, or treat the payment as made or presumed to be made to a foreign payee. With respect to payments through foreign intermediaries that are not qualified intermediaries (nonqualified intermediaries), brokers may rely on the beneficial owner's self-certification of non-U.S. status passed on by the nonqualified intermediary to determine whether certain third-party information reporting, and therefore backup withholding, may be required.

A withholding agent generally must withhold tax at a rate of 30 percent from the gross amount of all U.S.-source fixed or determinable annual or periodical gains, profits, or income (FDAP income) of a nonresident alien individual or foreign entity. FDAP income includes interest and dividends, but generally does not include gross proceeds or gains from sales. A foreign payee may claim a refund of any overpayment of tax which is withheld at source.

## Reasons for Change

U.S. persons seeking to evade U.S. tax may arrange to receive payments, with respect to which gross proceeds would otherwise be reported, through nonqualified intermediaries and certify that they qualify as foreign persons. A broker making a payment through a nonqualified intermediary is unlikely to be in a position to verify whether self-certification regarding foreign status is accurate. The proposal would discourage U.S. persons from attempting to evade U.S. tax by providing incorrect self-certification or otherwise relying on the lack of information reporting associated with using nonqualified intermediaries. The proposal would also encourage use of the strengthened qualified intermediary system by requiring withholding on gross proceeds on the sale of securities held through nonqualified intermediaries.

## Proposal

Under the proposal, a withholding agent would be required to withhold tax at a rate of 20 percent on gross proceeds from the sale of any security of a type that would be reported to a U.S. non-exempt payee, when paid by the withholding agent to a nonqualified intermediary that is located in a jurisdiction with which the United States does not have a comprehensive income tax treaty that includes a satisfactory exchange of information program. The Treasury Department would receive regulatory authority to provide exceptions, including exceptions for payments collected by nonqualified intermediaries for foreign government, central bank, foreign pension fund, and foreign insurance company payees, and other similar investors; payments to nonqualified intermediaries located in jurisdictions with which the United States has a tax information exchange agreement; and payments that the Treasury Department concludes present a low risk of tax evasion. The rules will be designed so as not to disrupt ordinary and customary market transactions. Nonqualified intermediaries would be eligible to claim a refund on behalf of their direct account holders for any taxable year in which they identified all of their direct account holders that are U.S. persons and reported all reportable payments received on behalf of U.S. account holders. Foreign persons that are subject to withholding tax in excess of their income tax liability as a result of this proposal, and on whose behalf a refund claim is not made by a nonqualified intermediary, would be permitted to apply for a refund of any tax withheld.

The proposal would be effective for payments made after December 31 of the year of enactment.

## REQUIRE REPORTING OF CERTAIN TRANSFERS OF MONEY OR PROPERTY TO FOREIGN FINANCIAL ACCOUNTS

### Current Law

United States persons must disclose whether, at any time during the preceding year, they had an interest in, or signature or other authority over, financial accounts in a foreign country, if the aggregate value of these accounts exceeds $10,000. United States persons must also report certain information with respect to certain foreign business entities that they control. Under Treasury regulations, a U.S. person controls a foreign corporation for this purpose if the person owns, actually or constructively, more than 50 percent of the corporation's stock, by vote or by value. Current law does not contain a provision that generally requires reporting of transfers of money or property to, or receipt of money or property from, a foreign bank, brokerage, or other financial account by U.S. individuals.

### Reason for Change

The Administration is concerned about the use of foreign accounts by U.S. citizens and residents to evade U.S. tax. To reduce such evasion, the Administration proposes to increase information reporting requirements with respect to transfers to and from certain foreign accounts.

### Proposal

A U.S. individual would be required to report, on the individual's income tax return, any transfer of money or property made to, or receipt of money or property from, any foreign bank, brokerage, or other financial account by the individual, or by any entity of which the individual owns, actually or constructively, more than 50 percent of the ownership interest. Transfers to accounts held at qualified intermediaries and receipts from accounts held by U.S. persons at qualified intermediaries would not be required to be reported. In addition, individuals would be exempt from the reporting requirement if the cumulative amount or value of transfers and the cumulative amount or value of receipts that would otherwise be reportable on the individual's income tax return for a given year were each less than $10,000. Failure to report a covered transfer would result in the imposition of a penalty equal to the lesser of $10,000 per reportable transfer or 10 percent of the cumulative amount or value of the unreported covered transfers. No penalty would be imposed for a failure to report due to reasonable cause. The Treasury Department would receive regulatory authority to issue rules to prevent abuse of the reporting exemptions and to provide exceptions to the reporting requirement, such as an exception for arm's-length payments in the ordinary course of business for services or tangible property.

The proposal would be effective for transfers made after December 31 of the year of enactment.

## REQUIRE DISCLOSURE OF FBAR ACCOUNTS TO BE FILED WITH TAX RETURN

### Current Law

Individual taxpayers currently must indicate on their income tax returns whether they had an interest in or signature or other authority over a financial account in a foreign country during the year to which the tax return relates. If a taxpayer has a foreign account, the tax return refers the taxpayer to the Report of Foreign Bank and Financial Accounts, Form TD F 90-22.1 (FBAR). The FBAR requires a citizen, resident, or person in and doing business in the United States to disclose whether, at any time during the preceding year, that person had an interest in, or signature authority over, financial accounts, if the aggregate value of these accounts exceeds $10,000. The FBAR further requires the person to disclose certain information regarding the foreign account, including the account number, financial institution, and maximum value during the year. The FBAR is not required to be filed until June 30 of the year following the calendar year to which it relates. The FBAR is filed with the Treasury Department generally and not directly with the IRS.

### Reasons for Change

Disclosure of more detailed information regarding foreign accounts on the income tax return itself would assist the IRS in identifying and investigating instances where taxpayers have used foreign accounts to evade U.S. taxes. Further, associating the FBAR disclosure requirements with a taxpayer's obligation to file an income tax return would improve awareness and compliance with the FBAR disclosure obligations and improve the IRS's ability to review FBAR compliance.

### Proposal

Individual taxpayers required to file an FBAR would be required to disclose certain information on their income tax returns. The information would be disclosed on a schedule that would be considered part of the individual's income tax return. The schedule would be consistent with the information disclosure obligations of the FBAR itself, and would require the taxpayer to provide information such as the account number, financial institution, and maximum value during the year. The disclosures would be required when the income tax return is due, even if Title 31 does not require the FBAR to be filed until a later date.

The tax return disclosure would not replace or mitigate the individual's obligation to separately file an FBAR with the Treasury Department as required under Title 31. The penalties imposed under Title 31 for failing to file an FBAR would continue to apply to a failure to file an FBAR as required under Title 31. Failure to disclose the foreign accounts with the income tax return would not be subject to the Title 31 penalties, although it could give rise to penalties and other consequences imposed under the Code, including extension of the statute of limitations.

The proposal would be effective for taxable years beginning after December 31 of the year of enactment.

**REQUIRE THIRD-PARTY INFORMATION REPORTING REGARDING THE TRANSFER OF ASSETS TO FOREIGN FINANCIAL ACCOUNTS AND THE ESTABLISHMENT OF FOREIGN FINANCIAL ACCOUNTS**

## Current Law

United States persons must disclose whether, at any time during the preceding year, they had an interest in, or signature or other authority over, financial accounts in a foreign country, if the aggregate value of these accounts exceeds $10,000. Current law does not generally require third-party information reporting to the IRS with regard to the transfer of money or property to, or receipt of money or property from, a foreign bank, brokerage, or other financial account on behalf of a U.S. person, or with regard to the establishment of a foreign bank, brokerage, or other financial account on behalf of a U.S. person.

## Reasons for Change

The Administration is concerned that U.S. persons are failing to comply with the requirement to report certain foreign financial accounts. Establishing a third-party reporting requirement with respect to transfers to foreign financial accounts, receipts from such accounts, and the establishment of such accounts would lead to greater disclosure of foreign financial accounts, and consequently would discourage the evasion of U.S. taxation. These third-party reporting requirements complement taxpayer reporting requirements.

## Proposal

Any U.S. financial intermediary and any qualified intermediary that transfers money or property with a value of more than $10,000 to a foreign bank, brokerage, or other financial account on behalf of a U.S. person (or on behalf of any entity of which a U.S. person owns, actually or constructively, more than 50 percent of the ownership interest) would be required to file an information return regarding such transfer. Any U.S. financial intermediary and any qualified intermediary that receives a transfer of money or property with a value of more than $10,000 from a foreign bank, brokerage, or other financial account on behalf of a U.S. person (or on behalf of any entity of which a U.S. person owns, actually or constructively, more than 50 percent of the ownership interest) would be required to file an information return regarding such transfer. Any U.S. financial intermediary and any qualified intermediary that opens a foreign bank, brokerage, or other financial account on behalf of a U.S. person (or on behalf of any entity of which a U.S. person owns, actually or constructively, more than 50 percent of the ownership interest) would be required to file an information return with the IRS regarding such account, including reporting any amounts of money or property transferred by the financial intermediary to such account. Exceptions to the reporting requirement would be provided for 1) accounts opened and amounts transferred to, from, or on behalf of, publicly traded companies and their subsidiaries, 2) accounts opened at and transfers made to qualified intermediaries on behalf of a U.S. person (or on behalf of any entity of which a U.S. person owns, actually or constructively, more than 50 percent of the ownership interest) or 3) transfers received by or on behalf of a U.S. person (or on behalf of any entity of which a U.S. person owns, actually or constructively, more than 50 percent of the ownership interest) from accounts held by a U.S. person at a qualified intermediary. The Treasury Department would receive regulatory authority to provide additional exceptions to the reporting requirement, to require that certain additional information be reported, and to permit U.S. financial intermediaries and qualified intermediaries to report additional transfers of money or property to a foreign bank, brokerage, or other financial account on behalf of a U.S. person (or on behalf of an entity of which the U.S. person owns, actually or constructively, more than 50 percent of the ownership interest).

The proposal would be effective for amounts transferred and accounts opened beginning after December 31 of the year of enactment.

# REQUIRE THIRD-PARTY INFORMATION REPORTING REGARDING THE ESTABLISHMENT OF OFFSHORE ENTITIES

## Current Law

United States persons must report certain information with respect to certain foreign business entities that they control. Current law does not generally require third-party information reporting in connection with the acquisition or formation of a foreign business entity on behalf of a U.S. individual. Current law does not require withholding agents to ascertain the ownership of foreign payees that may be entities with respect to which U.S. persons have a U.S. reporting or income tax obligation.

## Reasons for Change

Because no information is reported to the IRS by third parties with respect to the formation of foreign business entities, the IRS cannot readily ascertain whether U.S. individuals are complying with their reporting obligations in regard of foreign business entities that they control. Requiring third-party reporting, and providing for additional information collection by withholding agents, would supplement the reporting requirements of current law and help the IRS to enforce U.S. tax law and reduce tax evasion through the use of foreign entities.

## Proposal

Any U.S. person, or any qualified intermediary, that forms or acquires a foreign entity on behalf of a U.S. individual (or on behalf of any entity of which the individual owns, actually or constructively, more than 50 percent of the ownership interest) would be required to file an information return with the IRS regarding the foreign entity that is formed or acquired. The Treasury Department would receive regulatory authority to determine the information to be reported and to provide exceptions to the reporting requirement. In addition, the Treasury Department would receive regulatory authority to require, as necessary, withholding agents to collect additional information to determine whether a U.S. person is the beneficial owner of a foreign entity and specifically report if a U.S. person is a beneficial owner.

The proposal would be effective for entities formed or acquired after December 31 of the year of enactment.

## NEGATIVE PRESUMPTION FOR FOREIGN ACCOUNTS WITH RESPECT TO WHICH AN FBAR HAS NOT BEEN FILED

### Current Law

A citizen or resident of the United States, or a person in and doing business in the United States, who has a financial interest in, or signature or other authority over, financial accounts in a foreign country must file a Report of Foreign Bank and Financial Accounts (FBAR) if the aggregate value of these accounts exceeds $10,000 at any time during the preceding year. The civil penalty for failing to disclose a foreign financial account on an FBAR will not exceed $10,000 absent a willful violation. The penalty may not be imposed if the violation was due to reasonable cause and the balance in the account was properly reported. For willful violations, the maximum civil penalty is the greater of $100,000 or 50 percent of the balance in the account at the time of the violation. The criminal penalties for willfully failing to report a foreign bank account include a maximum fine of $250,000, a maximum term of imprisonment of five years, or both, with higher penalties if the defendant violates any other U.S. law, or if the violation was part of a pattern of any illegal activity involving more than $100,000 in a 12-month period. Civil and criminal penalties may be imposed together.

### Reasons for Change

The Administration is concerned that U.S. persons are failing to comply with FBAR filing obligations. Under current law, the civil penalty provisions associated with the requirement to file an FBAR may be difficult to apply in cases where the IRS is aware of the existence of unreported foreign financial accounts but cannot ascertain without documentation from the foreign financial institution whether those accounts contain more than $10,000. Imposing a rebuttable evidentiary presumption would encourage voluntary disclosure of account information and assist the IRS in its enforcement efforts with respect to undisclosed foreign financial accounts.

### Proposal

A rebuttable evidentiary presumption would be applicable in a civil administrative or judicial proceeding providing that any foreign bank, brokerage, or other financial account in which a citizen or resident of the United States, or a person in and doing business in the United States, has a financial interest in or signature or other authority over the account contains enough funds to require that an FBAR be filed. An exception would apply for accounts held through a qualified intermediary. The Treasury Department would receive regulatory authority to provide additional exceptions. The rebuttable evidentiary presumption would not apply in criminal proceedings.

The proposal would be effective for FBARs due to be filed beginning after the date of enactment.

## NEGATIVE PRESUMPTION REGARDING FAILURE TO FILE AN FBAR FOR ACCOUNTS WITH NONQUALIFIED INTERMEDIARIES

### Current Law

A citizen or resident of the United States, or a person in and doing business in the United States, who has a financial interest in, or signature or other authority over, financial accounts in a foreign country must file a Report of Foreign Bank and Financial Accounts (FBAR) if the aggregate value of these accounts exceeds $10,000 at any time during the preceding year. The civil penalty for failing to disclose a foreign financial account on an FBAR will not exceed $10,000 absent a willful violation. The penalty may not be imposed if the violation was due to reasonable cause and the balance in the account was properly reported. For willful violations, the maximum civil penalty is the greater of $100,000 or 50 percent of the balance in the account at the time of the violation. The criminal penalties for willfully failing to report a foreign bank account include a maximum fine of $250,000, a maximum term of imprisonment of five years, or both, with higher penalties if the defendant violates any other U.S. law, or if the violation was part of a pattern of any illegal activity involving more than $100,000 in a 12-month period. Civil and criminal penalties may be imposed together.

### Reasons for Change

The Administration is concerned that U.S. persons are failing to comply with FBAR filing obligations. Although qualified intermediaries must perform certain information reporting with respect to U.S. accountholders, foreign intermediaries that are not qualified intermediaries (nonqualified intermediaries) do not perform such information reporting. As a result, the ability of the IRS to discover unreported accounts and enforce compliance with respect to those accounts is limited. Imposing a rebuttable evidentiary presumption with respect to accounts held with nonqualified intermediaries would encourage voluntary disclosure of account information and assist the IRS in its enforcement efforts with respect to undisclosed foreign financial accounts.

### Proposal

A rebuttable evidentiary presumption would be applicable in a civil administrative or judicial proceeding providing that failure to file an FBAR with respect to any foreign bank, brokerage, or other financial account held with a nonqualified intermediary is willful if the account has a balance of greater than $200,000 at any point during the calendar year. The evidentiary presumption would not apply to accounts in which the person has signature or other authority by virtue of being an officer or employee of a corporation, but otherwise has no more than a de minimis financial interest in that corporation. The Treasury Department would receive regulatory authority to provide additional exceptions to the evidentiary presumption. The evidentiary presumption would not apply in criminal proceedings.

The proposal would be effective for FBARs due to be filed beginning after the date of enactment.

## NEGATIVE PRESUMPTION REGARDING WITHHOLDING ON FDAP PAYMENTS TO CERTAIN FOREIGN ENTITIES

### Current Law

In general, payments of U.S.-source fixed or determinable annual or periodical gains, profits, or income (FDAP income) to nonresident alien individuals and foreign entities are subject to withholding tax at a rate of 30 percent. This 30 percent withholding tax may be reduced or eliminated pursuant to certain statutory provisions or pursuant to the terms of a tax treaty.

To determine whether the recipient of a payment is exempt from withholding tax or eligible for a reduced rate, withholding agents generally must rely on beneficial ownership documentation provided by the payee certifying that the payee is entitled to an exemption from withholding tax or a reduced rate of withholding tax under a Code provision or relevant tax treaty. In general, withholding agents are entitled to rely on the self-certification they receive absent actual knowledge or reason to know that the information provided is incorrect or unreliable. In the case of payments made through an intermediary, the intermediary generally provides to the withholding agent the appropriate documentation on behalf of the payment's beneficial owners.

### Reasons for Change

Persons that are not entitled to an exemption from withholding tax or a reduced rate of withholding tax may arrange to receive payments through entities that appear to qualify for an exemption or a reduced rate. A withholding agent making a payment to such an entity is unlikely to be in a position to determine whether the entity's self-certification regarding its qualification is accurate.

### Proposal

Any withholding agent making a payment of FDAP income to a foreign entity would be required to treat the payment as made to an unknown person (and therefore subject to 30 percent gross-basis withholding tax), unless the foreign entity provides documentation of the entity's beneficial owners. Exceptions would be provided for payments to publicly traded companies and their subsidiaries, foreign governments, and pension funds. In addition, the Treasury Department would receive regulatory authority to provide additional exceptions for payments to entities engaged in the active conduct of a trade or business in their country of residence, charities, widely-held investment vehicles, entities that enter into an agreement with the IRS to collect documentation for all owners and report all U.S. non-exempt owners to the IRS, and for any other payment that the Treasury Department concludes presents a low risk of tax evasion.

The proposal would be effective for payments made after December 31 of the year of enactment.

# EXTEND STATUTE OF LIMITATIONS FOR CERTAIN REPORTABLE CROSS-BORDER TRANSACTIONS AND FOREIGN ENTITIES

## Current Law

In general, additional Federal tax liabilities in the form of tax, interest, penalties, and additions to tax must be assessed by the IRS within three years after the date a return is filed. If an assessment is not made within the required time period, the additional liabilities generally cannot be assessed or collected at any future time. Section 6501(c)(8) of the Code provides an exception to this general statute of limitations with respect to any tax relating to any event or period for which certain information returns are required with respect to certain foreign transfers, foreign entities, and foreign-owned entities. In these cases, the statute of limitations does not expire until three years after the taxpayer furnishes the information required to be reported.

Section 6038A of the Code requires certain foreign-owned domestic corporations to file information returns containing specified information with respect to related-party transactions, and to maintain such records as may be appropriate to determine the correct treatment of such transactions. Failure to file the required information returns triggers the section 6501(c)(8) extension of the statute of limitations.

## Reasons for Change

Compliance with reporting and recordkeeping obligations is essential in order to enable the IRS to enforce the tax laws. The three-year period provided by section 6501(c)(8) does not always allow sufficient time for the IRS to determine a taxpayer's tax liability. Furthermore, the information returns to which section 6501(c)(8) applies do not include some of the information returns the IRS requires in order to enforce the tax law with respect to foreign entities and accounts, including certain newly proposed information returns. The generally applicable three-year statute of limitations also does not always allow sufficient time for the IRS to determine a taxpayer's tax liability if a violation of record maintenance obligations under section 6038A has occurred.

## Proposal

The proposal would extend the period during which the statute of limitations provided by section 6501(c)(8) does not expire to six years after the taxpayer furnishes the information required to be reported. The information returns with respect to which section 6501(c)(8) applies would be broadened to include the information returns filed by qualifying electing funds pursuant to regulations under section 1295(b) of the Code, the proposed tax return disclosure of FBAR information, and the information returns proposed to be required of U.S. individuals with respect to certain transfers of money or property to and receipts from certain foreign bank, brokerage, or other financial accounts. The extended statute of limitations provided by section 6501(c)(8) would also apply in the case of failure to furnish information or maintain records as required by section 6038A(a). The section 6501(c)(8) exception to the general statute of limitations would be made applicable to the entire income tax return. The Treasury Department would receive regulatory authority to provide exceptions to these rules.

The proposal would be effective for returns due to be filed after the date of enactment.

## DOUBLE ACCURACY-RELATED PENALTIES ON UNDERSTATEMENTS INVOLVING UNDISCLOSED FOREIGN ACCOUNTS

### Current Law

Current law imposes a 20-percent accuracy-related penalty on (i) a substantial understatement of income tax, (ii) an understatement resulting from negligence or disregard of rules or regulations, and (iii) an understatement related to a reportable transaction. The 20-percent accuracy-related penalty increases to 30 percent in the case of an understatement from a reportable transaction that was not properly disclosed. The accuracy-related penalty is not imposed when the taxpayer demonstrates "reasonable cause" for the position and acted in good faith. In the case of a reportable transaction, the reasonable cause exception to the imposition of penalties only applies if the taxpayer disclosed the reportable transaction as required by law and certain other requirements are met.

Individual taxpayers must indicate on their income tax returns whether they had an interest in or signature or other authority over a financial account in a foreign country during the year to which the tax return relates. If the taxpayer had a foreign financial account, the income tax return instructs the taxpayer to refer to the Report of Foreign Bank and Financial Accounts (FBAR), which requires the taxpayer to disclose information regarding certain foreign accounts.

### Reason for Change

United States persons may seek to evade U.S. tax liability by transferring assets to foreign accounts. Increasing the penalties on understatements from transactions that involve undisclosed foreign accounts would encourage proper disclosure of such accounts and deter the use of foreign accounts to evade U.S. tax liability.

### Proposal

The 20-percent accuracy-related penalty imposed on (i) substantial understatements of income tax, (ii) understatements resulting from negligence or disregard of rules or regulations, or (iii) a reportable transaction understatement, would be doubled to 40 percent when the understatement arises from a transaction involving a foreign account that the taxpayer failed to disclose properly under the proposed requirement that taxpayers disclose FBAR-related information on their income tax returns. In addition, in the case of a reportable transaction understatement, the reasonable cause exception would not be available with respect to this increased penalty.

The proposal would be effective for taxable years beginning after December 31 of the year of enactment.

# IMPROVE THE FOREIGN TRUST REPORTING PENALTY

## Current Law

Certain information must be reported to the IRS with respect to certain foreign trusts. A civil penalty applies to persons who fail to file a timely return as required or who file an incomplete or incorrect return. Generally, the penalty is equal to 35 percent of the "gross reportable amount," which is defined as the gross value of property involved in a reportable event such as a gratuitous transfer to the trust, the gross value of the portion of the trust's assets at the close of the year that is treated as owned by a United States person, or the gross amount of distributions received from the trust. In the case of a failure to report that continues for more than 90 days after the IRS mails notice of such failure, the penalty (in addition to the 35 percent penalty) is $10,000 for each 30-day period (or fraction thereof) during which the failure continues. The total penalty with respect to any failure may not exceed the gross reportable amount.

## Reasons for Change

In many instances, the IRS obtains information relating to the creation of a foreign trust from third parties, or the IRS discovers funding of a foreign trust from public records. Without the cooperation of persons actually involved with the trust, however, it is often difficult for the IRS to determine the gross reportable amount. If the IRS cannot determine the gross reportable amount, the IRS may not be able to assess the penalties, including the $10,000 penalty for continued failure to report. The current penalty regime therefore may create an incentive for persons subject to the reporting requirement not to report or cooperate with the IRS in the hope that the IRS will not be able to determine the gross reportable amount, which is essential to presenting a prima facie case sufficient to meet the Code section 7491(c) burden of production to support the penalty.

## Proposal

The penalty provision would be amended to impose an initial penalty of the greater of $10,000 or 35 percent of the gross reportable amount (if the gross reportable amount is known). The additional $10,000 penalty for continued failure to report would remain unchanged. Thus, even if the gross reportable amount is not known, the IRS may impose a $10,000 penalty on a person who fails to report timely or correctly as required, and may impose a $10,000 penalty for each 30-day period (or fraction thereof) that the failure to report continues. If the person subsequently provides enough information for the IRS to determine the gross reportable amount, the total penalties would be capped at that amount and any excess penalty already paid would be refunded. Accordingly, a person can stop the compounding of penalties by cooperating with the IRS so that it can determine the gross reportable amount.

The proposal would be effective for information reports required to be filed after December 31 of the year of enactment.

**REQUIRE INFORMATION REPORTING FOR RENTAL PROPERTY EXPENSE PAYMENTS**

**Current Law**

Generally, a taxpayer making payments in the course of a trade or business to a noncorporate recipient aggregating to $600 or more for services or determinable gains in a calendar year is required to send an information return to the IRS setting forth the amount, as well as name and address of the recipient of the payment (generally on Form 1099). If the taxpayer making payments is not engaged in a trade or business, such information reporting is not required.

At present, there is limited third-party information reporting related to rental real estate expenses because only taxpayers whose rental real estate activity is considered a trade or business are required to report payments. Additionally, whether a taxpayer's rental real estate activity should be considered a trade or business requires a case-by-case analysis that depends on the facts and circumstances of each taxpayer.

**Reasons for Change**

Information reporting requirements generally improve taxpayer compliance. Requiring information reporting by taxpayers receiving rental income and deducting expenses on rental activities would improve the reporting compliance by taxpayers providing services to those rental activities. In addition, increased third-party reporting of major rental expenses is likely to improve reporting compliance on rental real estate income.

**Proposal**

The proposal would, in general, subject recipients of rental income from real estate would, in general, be subject to the same information reporting requirements as are taxpayers engaging in a trade or business. In particular, rental income recipients making payments of $600 or more to a service provider (such as a plumber, painter, or accountant) in the course of earning rental income would be required to send an information return, generally a Form 1099-MISC, to the IRS and to the service provider. Exceptions to the reporting requirement would be made for particularly burdensome situations, such as for taxpayers (including members of the military) who rent their principal residence on a temporary basis, or for those who receive only small amounts of rental income.

The proposal would be effective for tax years beginning after December 31, 2009.

**Eliminate Oil and Gas Company Preferences**

**LEVY TAX ON CERTAIN OFFSHORE OIL AND GAS PRODUCTION**

## Current Law

No Federal tax is imposed on the production of oil and gas on the Outer Continental Shelf (OCS).

## Reasons for Change

According to the Government Accountability Office, the return to the taxpayer from OCS production is among the lowest in the world, despite other factors that make the United States a comparatively good place to invest in oil and gas development. An excise tax on OCS production would advance important policy objectives, such as providing a more level playing field among producers, raising the return to the taxpayer, and encouraging sustainable domestic oil and gas production.

## Proposal

The Administration is developing a proposal to impose an excise tax on certain oil and gas produced offshore in the future. The Administration will work with Congress to develop the details of this proposal.

## REPEAL CREDIT FOR ENHANCED OIL RECOVERY (EOR) PROJECTS

### Current Law

The general business credit includes a 15-percent credit for eligible costs attributable to EOR projects. If the credit is claimed with respect to eligible costs, the taxpayer's deduction (or basis increase) with respect to those costs is reduced by the amount of the credit. Eligible costs include the cost of constructing a gas treatment plant to prepare Alaska natural gas for pipeline transportation and any of the following costs with respect to a qualified EOR project: (1) the cost of depreciable or amortizable tangible property that is an integral part of the project; (2) intangible drilling and development costs (IDCs) that the taxpayer can elect to deduct; and (3) deductible tertiary injectant costs. A qualified EOR project must be located in the United States and must involve the application of one or more of nine listed tertiary recovery methods that can reasonably be expected to result in more than an insignificant increase in the amount of crude oil which ultimately will be recovered. The allowable credit is phased out over a $6 range for a taxable year if the annual average unregulated wellhead price per barrel of domestic crude oil during the calendar year preceding the calendar year in which the taxable year begins (the reference price) exceeds an inflation adjusted threshold. The credit was completely phased out for taxable years beginning in 2008, because the reference price ($66.52) exceeded the inflation adjusted threshold ($41.06) by more than $6.

### Reasons for Change

The credit, like other oil and gas preferences the Administration proposes to repeal, distorts markets by encouraging more investment in the oil and gas industry than would occur under a neutral system. To the extent the credit encourages overproduction of oil, it is detrimental to long-term energy security and is also inconsistent with the Administration's policy of reducing carbon emissions and encouraging the use of renewable energy sources through a cap-and-trade program. Moreover, the credit must ultimately be financed with taxes that result in underinvestment in other, potentially more productive, areas of the economy.

### Proposal

The investment tax credit for enhanced oil recovery projects would be repealed for taxable years beginning after December 31, 2010.

# REPEAL CREDIT FOR PRODUCTION FROM MARGINAL WELLS

## Current Law

The general business credit includes a credit for crude oil and natural gas produced from marginal wells. The credit rate is $3.00 per barrel of oil and $0.50 per 1,000 cubic feet of natural gas for taxable years beginning in 2005 and is adjusted for inflation in taxable years beginning after 2005. The credit is available for production from wells that produce oil and gas qualifying as marginal production for purposes of the percentage depletion rules or that have average daily production of not more than 25 barrel-of-oil equivalents and produce at least 95 percent water. The credit per well is limited to 1,095 barrels of oil or barrel-of-oil equivalents per year. The credit rate for crude oil is phased out for a taxable year if the annual average unregulated wellhead price per barrel of domestic crude oil during the calendar year preceding the calendar year in which the taxable year begins (the reference price) exceeds the applicable threshold. The phase-out range and the applicable threshold at which phase-out begins are $3.00 and $15.00 for taxable years beginning in 2005 and are adjusted for inflation in taxable years beginning after 2005. The credit rate for natural gas is similarly phased out for a taxable year if the annual average wellhead price for domestic natural gas exceeds the applicable threshold. The phase-out range and the applicable threshold at which phase-out begins are $0.33 and $1.67 for taxable years beginning in 2005 and are adjusted for inflation in taxable years beginning after 2005. The credit has been completely phased out for all taxable years since its enactment. Unlike other components of the general business credit, the marginal well credit can be carried back up to five years.

## Reasons for Change

The credit, like other oil and gas preferences the Administration proposes to repeal, distorts markets by encouraging more investment in the oil and gas industry than would occur under a neutral system. To the extent the credit encourages overproduction of oil, it is detrimental to long-term energy security and is also inconsistent with the Administration's policy of reducing carbon emissions and encouraging the use of renewable energy sources through a cap-and-trade program. Moreover, the credit must ultimately be financed with taxes that result in underinvestment in other, potentially more productive, areas of the economy.

## Proposal

The production tax credit for oil and gas from marginal wells would be repealed for production in taxable years beginning after December 31, 2010.

## REPEAL EXPENSING OF INTANGIBLE DRILLING COSTS

### Current Law

In general, costs that benefit future periods must be capitalized and recovered over such periods for income tax purposes, rather than being expensed in the period the costs are incurred. In addition, the uniform capitalization rules require certain direct and indirect costs allocable to property to be included in inventory or capitalized as part of the basis of such property. In general, the uniform capitalization rules apply to real and tangible personal property produced by the taxpayer or acquired for resale.

Special rules apply to intangible drilling and development costs (IDCs). IDCs include all expenditures made by an operator for wages, fuel, repairs, hauling, supplies, etc., incident to and necessary for the drilling of wells and the preparation of wells for the production of oil and gas. In addition, IDCs include the cost to operators of any drilling or development work (excluding amounts payable only out of production or gross or net proceeds from production, if the amounts are depletable income to the recipient, and amounts properly allocable to the cost of depreciable property) done by contractors under any form of contract (including a turnkey contract). IDCs include amounts paid for labor, fuel, repairs, hauling, and supplies which are used in the drilling, shooting, and cleaning of wells; in such clearing of ground, draining, road making, surveying, and geological works as are necessary in preparation for the drilling of wells; and in the construction of such derricks, tanks, pipelines, and other physical structures as are necessary for the drilling of wells and the preparation of wells for the production of oil and gas. Generally, IDCs do not include expenses for items which have a salvage value (such as pipes and casings) or items which are part of the acquisition price of an interest in the property.

Under the special rules applicable to IDCs, an operator (i.e., a person who holds a working or operating interest in any tract or parcel of land either as a fee owner or under a lease or any other form of contract granting working or operating rights) who pays or incurs IDCs in the development of an oil or gas property located in the United States may elect either to expense or capitalize those costs. The uniform capitalization rules do not apply to otherwise deductible IDCs.

If a taxpayer elects to expense IDCs, the amount of the IDCs is deductible as an expense in the taxable year the cost is paid or incurred. Generally, IDCs that a taxpayer elects to capitalize may be recovered through depletion or depreciation, as appropriate; or in the case of a nonproductive well ("dry hole"), the operator may elect to deduct the costs. In the case of an integrated oil company (i.e., a company that engages, either directly or through a related enterprise, in substantial retailing or refining activities) that has elected to expense IDCs, 30 percent of the IDCs on productive wells must be capitalized and amortized over a 60-month period.

A taxpayer that has elected to deduct IDCs may, nevertheless, elect to capitalize and amortize certain IDCs over a 60-month period beginning with the month the expenditure was paid or incurred. This rule applies on an expenditure-by-expenditure basis; that is, for any particular taxable year, a taxpayer may deduct some portion of its IDCs and capitalize the rest under this provision. This allows the taxpayer to reduce or eliminate IDC adjustments or preferences under the AMT.

The election to deduct IDCs applies only to those IDCs associated with domestic properties. For this purpose, the United States includes certain wells drilled offshore.

## Reasons for Change

The expensing of IDCs, like other oil and gas preferences the Administration proposes to repeal, distorts markets by encouraging more investment in the oil and gas industry than would occur under a neutral system. To the extent expensing encourages overproduction of oil and gas, it is detrimental to long-term energy security and is also inconsistent with the Administration's policy of reducing carbon emissions and encouraging the use of renewable energy sources through a cap-and-trade program. Moreover, the tax subsidy for oil and gas must ultimately be financed with taxes that result in underinvestment in other, potentially more productive, areas of the economy. Capitalization of IDCs would place them on a cost recovery system similar to that employed by other industries and reduce economic distortions.

## Proposal

Expensing of intangible drilling costs and 60-month amortization of capitalized intangible drilling costs would not be allowed. Intangible drilling costs would be capitalized as depreciable or depletable property, depending on the nature of the cost incurred, in accordance with the generally applicable rules.

The proposal would be effective for costs paid or incurred after December 31, 2010.

**REPEAL DEDUCTION FOR TERTIARY INJECTANTS**

## Current Law

Taxpayers are allowed to deduct the cost of qualified tertiary injectant expenses for the taxable year. Qualified tertiary injectant expenses are amounts paid or incurred for any tertiary injectant (other than recoverable hydrocarbon injectants) that is used as a part of a tertiary recovery method. The deduction is treated as an amortization deduction in determining the amount subject to recapture upon disposition of the property.

## Reasons for Change

The deduction for tertiary injectants, like other oil and gas preferences the Administration proposes to repeal, distorts markets by encouraging more investment in the oil and gas industry than would occur under a neutral system. To the extent expensing encourages overproduction of oil and gas, it is detrimental to long-term energy security and is also inconsistent with the Administration's policy of reducing carbon emissions and encouraging the use of renewable energy sources through a cap-and-trade program. Moreover, the tax subsidy for oil and gas must ultimately be financed with taxes that result in underinvestment in other, potentially more productive, areas of the economy. Capitalization of tertiary injectants would place them on a cost recovery system similar to that employed by other industries and reduce economic distortions.

## Proposal

The deduction for qualified tertiary injectant expenses would not be allowed for amounts paid or incurred after December 31, 2010.

## REPEAL PASSIVE LOSS EXCEPTION FOR WORKING INTERESTS IN OIL AND GAS PROPERTIES

### Current Law

The passive loss rules limit deductions and credits from passive trade or business activities. Deductions attributable to passive activities, to the extent they exceed income from passive activities, generally may not be deducted against other income, such as wages, portfolio income, or business income that is not derived from a passive activity. A similar rule applies to credits. Suspended deductions and credits are carried forward and treated as deductions and credits from passive activities in the next year. The suspended losses and credits from a passive activity are allowed in full when the taxpayer completely disposes of the activity.

Passive activities are defined to include trade or business activities in which the taxpayer does not materially participate. An exception is provided, however, for any working interest in an oil or gas property that the taxpayer holds directly or through an entity that does not limit the liability of the taxpayer with respect to the interest.

### Reasons for Change

The special tax treatment of working interests in oil and gas properties, like other oil and gas preferences the Administration proposes to repeal, distorts markets by encouraging more investment in the oil and gas industry than would occur under a neutral system. To the extent this special treatment encourages overproduction of oil and gas, it is detrimental to long-term energy security and is also inconsistent with the Administration's policy of reducing carbon emissions and encouraging the use of renewable energy sources through a cap-and-trade program. Moreover, the working interest exception for oil and gas must ultimately be financed with taxes that result in underinvestment in other, potentially more productive, areas of the economy. Eliminating the working interest exception would subject oil and gas properties to the same limitations as other activities and reduce economic distortions.

### Proposal

The exception from the passive loss rules for working interests in oil and gas properties would be repealed for taxable years beginning after December 31, 2010.

## REPEAL PERCENTAGE DEPLETION

### Current Law

The capital costs of oil and gas wells are recovered through the depletion deduction. Under the cost depletion method, the basis recovery for a taxable year is proportional to the exhaustion of the property during the year. This method does not permit cost recovery deductions that exceed basis or that are allowable on an accelerated basis.

A taxpayer may also qualify for percentage depletion with respect to oil and gas properties. The amount of the deduction is a statutory percentage of the gross income from the property. For oil and gas properties, the percentage ranges from 15 to 25 percent and the deduction may not exceed 100 percent of the taxable income from the property. In addition, the percentage depletion deduction for oil and gas properties may not exceed 65 percent of the taxpayer's overall taxable income (determined before the deduction and with certain other adjustments).

Other limitations and special rules apply to the percentage depletion deduction for oil and gas properties. In general, only independent producers and royalty owners (as contrasted to integrated oil companies) qualify for the percentage depletion deduction. In addition, oil and gas producers may claim percentage depletion only with respect to up to 1,000 barrels of average daily production of domestic crude oil or an equivalent amount of domestic natural gas (applied on a combined basis in the case of taxpayers that produce both). This quantity limitation is allocated, at the taxpayer's election, between oil and gas production and then further allocated within each class among the taxpayer's properties. Special rules apply to oil and gas production from marginal wells (generally, wells for which the average daily production is less than 15 barrels of oil or barrel-of-oil equivalents or that produce only heavy oil). Only marginal well production can qualify for percentage depletion at a rate of more than 15 percent. The rate is increased in a taxable year that begins a calendar year following a calendar year during which the annual average unregulated wellhead price per barrel of domestic crude oil is less than $20 by one percentage point for each whole dollar of difference between the two amounts. In addition, marginal wells are exempt from the 100-percent-of-net-income limitation described above in taxable years beginning during the period 1998- 2007 and in taxable years beginning in 2009. Unless the taxpayer elects otherwise, marginal well production is given priority over other production in applying the 1,000-barrel limitation on percentage depletion.

A qualifying taxpayer determines the depletion deduction for each oil and gas property under both the percentage depletion method and the cost depletion method and deducts the larger of the two amounts. Because percentage depletion is computed without regard to the taxpayer's basis in the depletable property, a taxpayer may continue to claim percentage depletion after all the expenditures incurred to acquire and develop the property have been recovered.

### Reasons for Change

Percentage depletion effectively provides a lower rate of tax with respect to a favored source of income. The lower rate of tax, like other oil and gas preferences the Administration proposes to repeal, distorts markets by encouraging more investment in the oil and gas industry than would occur under a neutral system. To the extent the lower tax rate encourages overproduction of oil and gas, it is detrimental to long-term energy security and is also inconsistent with the Administration's policy of reducing carbon emissions and encouraging the use of renewable energy sources through a cap-and-trade program. Moreover, the tax subsidy for oil and gas must ultimately be financed with taxes that result in underinvestment in other, potentially more productive, areas of the economy.

Cost depletion computed by reference to the taxpayer's basis in the property is the equivalent of economic depreciation. Limiting oil and gas producers to cost depletion would place them on a cost recovery system similar to that employed by other industries and reduce economic distortions.

**Proposal**

Percentage depletion would not be allowed with respect to oil and gas wells. Taxpayers would be permitted to claim cost depletion on their adjusted basis, if any, in oil and gas wells.

The proposal would be effective for taxable years beginning after December 31, 2010.

# REPEAL DOMESTIC MANUFACTURING DEDUCTION FOR OIL AND GAS PRODUCTION

## Current Law

A deduction is allowed with respect to income attributable to domestic production activities (the manufacturing deduction). For taxable years beginning in 2009, the manufacturing deduction is equal to 6 percent of the lesser of qualified production activities income for the taxable year or taxable income for the taxable year, limited to 50-percent of the W-2 wages of the taxpayer for the taxable year. For taxable years beginning after 2009, the deduction is computed at a 9 percent rate, except that the deduction for income oil and gas production activities is computed at a 6 percent rate.

Qualified production activities income is generally calculated as a taxpayer's domestic production gross receipts (i.e., the gross receipts derived from any lease, rental, license, sale, exchange, or other disposition of qualifying production property manufactured, produced, grown, or extracted by the taxpayer in whole or significant part within the U.S.; any qualified film produced by the taxpayer; or electricity, natural gas, or potable water produced by the taxpayer in the U.S.) minus the cost of goods sold and other expenses, losses, or deductions attributable to such receipts.

The manufacturing deduction generally is available to all taxpayers that generate qualified production activities income, which under current law includes income from the sale, exchange or disposition of oil, natural gas or primary products produced in the United States.

## Reasons for Change

The manufacturing deduction effectively provides a lower rate of tax with respect to a favored source of income. The lower rate of tax, like other oil and gas preferences the Administration proposes to repeal, distorts markets by encouraging more investment in the oil and gas industry than would occur under a neutral system. To the extent the lower tax rate encourages overproduction of oil and gas, it is detrimental to long-term energy security and is also inconsistent with the Administration's policy of reducing carbon emissions and encouraging the use of renewable energy sources through a cap-and-trade program. Moreover, the tax subsidy for oil and gas must ultimately be financed with taxes that result in underinvestment in other, potentially more productive, areas of the economy.

## Proposal

The proposal would exclude from the definition of domestic production gross receipts all gross receipts derived from the sale, exchange or other disposition of oil, natural gas or a primary product thereof for taxable years beginning after December 31, 2010.

## INCREASE THE AMORTIZATION PERIOD FOR GEOLOGICAL AND GEOPHYSICAL COSTS TO SEVEN YEARS

### Current Law

Geological and geophysical expenditures are costs incurred for the purpose of obtaining and accumulating data that will serve as the basis for the acquisition and retention of mineral properties. The amortization period for geological and geophysical expenditures incurred in connection with oil and gas exploration in the United States is two years for independent producers and seven years for integrated oil and gas producers.

### Reasons for Change

The accelerated amortization of geological and geophysical expenditures incurred by independent producers, like other oil and gas preferences the Administration proposes to repeal, distorts markets by encouraging more investment in the oil and gas industry than would occur under a neutral system. To the extent accelerated amortization encourages overproduction of oil and gas, it is actually detrimental to long-term energy security and is also inconsistent with the Administration's policy of reducing carbon emissions and encouraging the use of renewable energy sources through a cap-and-trade program. Moreover, the tax subsidy for oil and gas must ultimately be financed with taxes that result in underinvestment in other, potentially more productive, areas of the economy.

Increasing the amortization period for geological and geophysical expenditures incurred by independent oil and gas producers from two years to seven years would provide a more accurate reflection of their income and more consistent tax treatment for all oil and gas producers.

### Proposal

The proposal would increase the amortization period from two years to seven years for geological and geophysical expenditures incurred by independent producers in connection with all oil and gas exploration in the United States. Seven-year amortization would apply even if the property is abandoned and any remaining basis of the abandoned property would be recovered over the remainder of the seven-year period. The proposal would be effective for amounts paid or incurred after December 31, 2010.

# ELIMINATE THE ADVANCED EARNED INCOME TAX CREDIT

## Current Law

Under current law, low- and moderate-income individuals may be eligible for the refundable EITC. The amount of EITC an eligible individual may claim is a function of income and earnings, the number of children in the household, and filing status. In 2009, families with one child are eligible for a maximum EITC of $3,043. Eligible individuals with more children receive a larger credit.

Since 1978, most eligible individuals have had the option of requesting advance payments of the EITC from their employers throughout the year. Self-employed and childless individuals are not eligible. Under current law, the advance payment is limited to 60 percent of the maximum credit to which a worker with one child would be entitled. In 2009, the maximum advance payment is $1,826.

Employers offset the costs of the advance payments by reducing their payments of withheld income and employment taxes. During the year, employers periodically notify the IRS of the aggregate amount of advance payments withheld from tax payments. After the tax year is over, the employer notifies the IRS of employees' receipts of advance payments. The information is also provided to the employees. Upon filing their tax returns, individuals must reconcile any advance payments received during the year with the amount of EITC for which they actually were eligible. If they received too little, they can obtain the remaining amount; conversely, if they received too much, they must repay the overpayment with their tax return. Individuals who have received an advance payment are required to file a tax return, even if their income is below the filing threshold. In view of the risk of overpayments, the advance payment is limited to 60 percent of the one-child maximum credit.

## Reason for Change

The advance payment option provides a mechanism for individuals to receive payments on a timely basis, instead of as a single payment during the filing season. Advance payments could help cash-constrained households meet their daily needs. However, advance payments have been extremely unpopular among eligible taxpayers – at most, 3 percent of eligible individuals participate, and IRS' efforts to increase participation have not had a meaningful impact. Furthermore, recent research shows evidence of significant non-compliance by employers and workers. As a consequence, repealing the advance payment option would affect adversely few individuals who are eligible for this benefit.

## Proposal

The proposal would repeal the advance payment option of the EITC. Workers would no longer be able to receive an advance against their expected EITC through their employer. (Individuals with positive tax liability would still be able to receive any non-refundable portion of the EITC during the year through adjustments in their withholding.)

The proposal would be effective for taxable years beginning after December 31, 2009.

# UPPER-INCOME TAX PROVISIONS DEDICATED TO DEFICIT REDUCTION

## REINSTATE THE 39.6-PERCENT RATE

### Current Law

Prior to the enactment of EGTRRA, the highest individual income tax rate was 39.6-percent. EGTRRA reduced the 39.6-percent tax rate temporarily to 35 percent, with the reduction phased in over several years.  The Jobs and Growth Tax Relief Reconciliation Act of 2003 (JGTRRA) accelerated the reduction, and since 2003, the highest statutory individual income tax rate has been 35 percent.  For 2009, it applies to taxable income over $372,950 ($186,475 if married filing separately).  The 35-percent tax rate sunsets after 2010.

### Reason for Change

Increasing the income tax liability of wealthy taxpayers would make the income tax system more progressive and would distribute the cost of government more fairly among taxpayers of various income levels.

### Proposal

The Administration's tax receipts baseline would permanently extend the EGTRRA tax rates. This proposal would permit the EGTRRA reduction in the highest income tax rate to sunset after 2010.  Thus, beginning in 2011, the highest income tax rate would be 39.6 percent.  The taxable income levels at which this rate begins to apply would vary by filing status and would be indexed annually for inflation.

**REINSTATE THE 36-PERCENT RATE FOR TAXPAYERS WITH INCOME OVER $250,000 (MARRIED FILING A JOINT RETURN) AND $200,000 (SINGLE)**

## Current Law

Prior to the enactment of EGTRRA, the second highest individual income tax rate was 36 percent. EGTRRA reduced the 36-percent tax rate temporarily to 33 percent, with the reduction phased in over several years. JGTRRA accelerated the reduction, and since 2003, the second highest statutory individual income tax rate has been 33 percent. In 2009, it applies to taxable income over $208,850 if married filing jointly ($171,550 if single). The 33-percent tax rate sunsets after 2010.

## Reason for Change

Increasing the income tax liability of wealthy taxpayers would make the income tax system more progressive and would distribute the cost of government more fairly among taxpayers of various income levels.

## Proposal

The Administration's tax receipts baseline would permanently extend the EGTRRA tax rates. This proposal would permit the EGTRRA reduction in the second highest income tax rate to sunset after 2010. Thus, beginning in 2011, the second highest tax rate would be 36 percent. The taxable income levels at which that rate begins to apply would vary by filing status and would be indexed annually for inflation. The 36-percent tax rate would apply to taxable income above the following amounts but less than the income levels at which the 39.6-percent rate would apply: $250,000 less the standard deduction and two personal exemptions, indexed from 2009, for married taxpayers filing jointly; $200,000 less the standard deduction and one personal exemption, indexed from 2009, for single filers. The 28-percent tax rate bracket would be expanded so that taxpayers earning less than these amounts would not see their taxes rise as a result of the increased tax rate brackets.

# REINSTATE THE LIMITATION ON ITEMIZED DEDUCTIONS FOR TAXPAYERS WITH INCOME OVER $250,000 (MARRIED FILING A JOINT RETURN) AND $200,000 (SINGLE)

## Current Law

Individual taxpayers may elect to itemize their deductions instead of claiming a standard deduction. In general, itemized deductions include medical and dental expenses (in excess of 7.5 percent of AGI), state and local property taxes and either income or sales taxes, interest paid, gifts to charities, casualty and theft losses (in excess of 10 percent of AGI), job expenses and certain miscellaneous expenses (some only in excess of 2 percent of AGI).

Prior to the enactment of EGTRRA, otherwise allowable itemized deductions (other than medical expenses, investment interest, theft and casualty losses, and gambling losses) were reduced by 3 percent of the amount by which AGI exceeded a statutory floor that was indexed annually for inflation, but not by more than 80 percent of the otherwise allowable deductions. EGTRRA reduced the itemized deduction limitation in three steps. For 2006 and 2007, itemized deductions were reduced by 2 percent of AGI over the threshold, but not by more than 53-1/3 percent. For 2008 and 2009, itemized deductions were reduced by 1 percent of AGI over the threshold, but not by more than 26-2/3 percent. For 2010, the reduction was to be completely eliminated. However, beginning in 2011, the full itemized deduction reduction of 3 percent of AGI exceeding the floor is scheduled to be reinstated.

For 2009, the AGI floor is $166,800 ($83,400 if married filing separately).

## Reason for Change

By limiting the tax benefit of higher-income taxpayers' itemized deductions, the income tax system would be made more progressive and the cost of government would be shared more fairly by taxpayers in all levels of income.

## Proposal

The Administration's tax receipts baseline would permanently extend the EGTRRA repeal of the limitation on itemized deductions. This proposal would allow the elimination of the limitation on itemized deduction enacted in EGTRRA to sunset after 2010. Thus, itemized deductions (other than medical expenses, investment interest, theft and casualty losses, and gambling losses) would be reduced by 3 percent of the amount by which AGI exceeds statutory floors which are higher than under current law, but not by more than 80 percent of the otherwise allowable deductions. The floors would be indexed annually for inflation. For 2011, the AGI floors would be adjusted for inflation starting with a value of $250,000 in 2009 for married taxpayers filing jointly and $200,000 in 2009 for single taxpayers.

**REINSTATE THE PERSONAL EXEMPTION PHASE-OUT (PEP) FOR TAXPAYERS WITH INCOME OVER $250,000 (MARRIED FILING A JOINT RETURN) AND $200,000 (SINGLE)**

## Current Law

Individual taxpayers generally are entitled to a personal exemption for the taxpayer and for each dependent. The amount of each personal exemption is $3,650 for 2009 and is indexed annually for inflation.

Prior to the enactment of EGTRRA, all personal exemptions were reduced or completely phased out simultaneously for higher-income taxpayers. For a taxpayer with AGI in excess of the threshold amount for the taxpayer's filing status, the amount of each personal exemption was reduced by 2 percent of the exemption amount for that year for each $2,500 ($1,250 if married filing separately) or fraction thereof by which AGI exceeded that threshold. EGTRRA reduced the otherwise applicable reduction of personal exemptions by one-third for 2006 and 2007, by two-thirds for 2008 and 2009, and eliminated it completely for 2010. However, beginning in 2011, the full personal exemption phase-out is scheduled to be reinstated.

For 2009, personal exemptions are reduced by 0.6667 percentage points for each $2,500 ($1,250 if married filing separately) or fraction thereof by which AGI exceeds the threshold, but not by more than one-third of the unreduced exemption amount. Thus, even the highest-income taxpayers are entitled to claim $2,433.33 for each personal exemption. For 2009, the thresholds at which personal exemptions begin to be reduced if AGI exceeds these amounts are $166,800 for single taxpayers, $208,500 for heads of household, $250,200 for married taxpayers filing jointly, and $125,100 for married taxpayers filing separately.

## Reason for Change

By limiting the tax benefit of higher-income taxpayers' personal exemptions, the income tax system would be made more progressive, and the cost of government would be shared more fairly by taxpayers in all levels of income.

## Proposal

The Administration's tax receipts baseline would permanently extend the EGTRRA repeal of the personal exemption phase-out. This proposal would allow the elimination of the personal exemption phase-out enacted in EGTRRA to sunset after 2010. The AGI levels at which the phase-out begins would be adjusted. For 2011, the AGI floors would be adjusted for inflation starting with a value of $250,000 in 2009 for married taxpayers filing jointly ($125,000 if filing separately) and $200,000 in 2009 for single taxpayers.

**IMPOSE A 20-PERCENT RATE ON DIVIDENDS AND CAPITAL GAINS FOR TAXPAYERS WITH INCOME OVER $250,000 (MARRIED FILING A JOINT RETURN) AND $200,000 (SINGLE)**

## Current Law

A separate rate structure applies to long-term capital gains and dividends. Under current law, the maximum rate of tax on the adjusted net capital gain of an individual is 15 percent. In addition, any adjusted net capital gain otherwise taxed at a 10- or 15-percent rate is taxed at a zero-percent rate. These rates apply for purposes of both the regular tax and the AMT. Qualified dividends generally are taxed at the same rate as capital gains.

Capital losses generally are deductible in full against capital gains. In addition, individual taxpayers may deduct up to $3,000 of capital losses from ordinary income in each year. Any remaining unused capital losses may be carried forward indefinitely to a future year.

The zero- and 15-percent rates for dividends and capital gains are scheduled to sunset for taxable years beginning after December 31, 2010. In 2011, the maximum rate on capital gains would increase to 20 percent, while the tax rates for dividends would go back to the higher ordinary tax rates of up to 39.6 percent.

## Reasons for Change

The Administration supports keeping income tax rates low on corporate dividends and capital gains (including sales and exchanges of corporate stock). Lower- and middle-income taxpayers should be protected from the tax increase that would otherwise occur in 2011. Allowing the 15-percent rate to expire for high-income taxpayers who are most able to absorb it would still keep the top rate at historically low levels. The 20-percent maximum rate on capital gains would be the same as the maximum capital gains rate enacted in 1987, and is the same as the top rate enacted in 1981. Taxing qualified dividends at the same low rate as capital gains reduces the tax bias against equity investment and helps promote more efficient allocation of capital since investors can choose to reallocate their dividends to the most productive investments.

## Proposal

The Administration's tax receipts baseline would permanently extend the zero- and 15-percent tax rates for dividends and capital gains. The zero- and 15-percent tax rates for capital gains and qualified dividends would be extended permanently for taxpayers with incomes up to $250,000 for joint returns and $200,000 for single taxpayers. The 20-percent tax rate on long-term capital gains and qualified dividends would apply for married taxpayers filing jointly with income over $250,000 less the standard deduction and two personal exemptions (indexed from 2009) and for single taxpayers with income over $200,000 less the standard deduction and one personal exemption (indexed from 2009). The reduced rates on gains on assets held over 5 years would be repealed.

This proposal is effective on the date of enactment for taxable years beginning after December 31, 2010.

# USER FEES

## PRESERVE COST-SHARING OF INLAND WATERWAYS CAPITAL COSTS

### Current Law

The Inland Waterways Trust Fund is supported by a 20-cents-per-gallon tax on liquids used as fuel in a vessel in commercial waterway transportation. Commercial waterway transportation is defined as any use of a vessel on any inland or intracoastal waterway of the United States (1) in the business of transporting property for compensation or hire or (2) in the business of the owner, lessee, or operator of the vessel (other than fish or other aquatic animal life caught on the voyage). The inland or intracoastal waterways of the United States are the inland and intracoastal waterways of the United States described in section 206 of the Inland Waterways Revenue Act of 1978. Exceptions are provided for deep-draft ocean-going vessels, passenger vessels, State and local governments, and certain ocean-going barges.

### Reasons for Change

The fuel excise tax does not raise enough revenue to pay for the users' 50-percent share of the capital costs of the locks and dams that make barge transportation possible on inland and intracoastal waterways. Moreover, the tax is not the most efficient method for financing expenditures on those waterways. Adequate funding for inland and intracoastal waterways can be provided through a more efficient user fee system that is based on lock usage and is tied to the level of spending for inland waterways construction, replacement, expansion, and rehabilitation work.

### Proposal

The tax on liquids used as fuel in a vessel in commercial waterway transportation would be phased out and replaced by a fee system based on lock usage. The tax rate would be reduced to 10 cents per gallon beginning January 1, 2012. The tax would be repealed for periods after December 31, 2013. The fee system based on lock usage would be phased in beginning on January 1, 2010. For calendar year 2014 and each subsequent calendar year, the fee schedule would be adjusted as necessary to maintain an appropriate level of net assets in the Inland Waterways Trust Fund.

# OTHER INITIATIVES

## IMPLEMENT UNEMPLOYMENT INSURANCE INTEGRITY LEGISLATION

### Current Law

The Federal Unemployment Tax Act (FUTA) currently imposes a Federal payroll tax on employers of 6.2 percent of the first $7,000 paid annually to each employee. Generally, these funds support the administrative costs of the unemployment insurance system. Employers in States that meet certain Federal requirements are allowed a credit against FUTA taxes of up to 5.4 percent, making the minimum net Federal rate 0.8 percent. States also impose an unemployment tax on employers. A State's unemployment insurance taxes are first placed in the State's own clearing account and then deposited into its Federal unemployment insurance trust fund account from which the State pays unemployment benefits. State recoveries of overpayments of unemployment insurance benefits must be similarly deposited and used exclusively to pay unemployment benefits.

While States may assess penalties for overpayments of benefits, amounts collected as penalties or interest on benefit overpayments may be treated as general receipts by the States.

### Reasons for Change

States' abilities to reduce benefit overpayments and increase overpayment recoveries are limited by funding. The mandatory redeposit of the collection of all unemployment benefits overpayments prevents States from redirecting some of these amounts to future recovery activity. Although States might use penalties or interest on overpayments to increase collections, there is no requirement that such amounts be directed for additional enforcement activities.

### Proposal

The proposal would increase resources for the recovery of State unemployment benefit overpayments and delinquent employer taxes. The proposal would allow States to redirect up to 5 percent of overpayment recoveries to additional enforcement activity. The proposal would require States to impose a penalty of at least 15 percent on recipients of fraudulent overpayments, and penalty revenue would be used exclusively for additional enforcement activity. The proposal would expand the ability to collect benefit overpayments due to a State from income tax refunds owed to a benefit recipient. The proposal would allow States to deposit up to 5 percent of moneys recovered in the course of an unemployment insurance tax investigation into a special fund dedicated to implementing the State Unemployment Tax Act (SUTA) Dumping Prevention Act of 2004 or enforcing State laws relating to employer fraud or tax evasion. The proposal would require employers to report a "start work date" to the National Directory of New Hires for all new hires.

The proposal would be effective upon the date of enactment.

**Restructure Assistance to New York City**

## PROVIDE TAX INCENTIVES FOR TRANSPORTATION INFRASTRUCTURE

### Current Law

The Job Creation and Worker Assistance Act of 2002 (the Act) provided tax incentives for the area of New York City damaged or affected by the terrorist attacks on September 11, 2001. The Act created the "New York Liberty Zone," defined as the area located on or south of Canal Street, East Broadway (east of its intersection with Canal Street), or Grand Street (east of its intersection with East Broadway) in the Borough of Manhattan in the City of New York, New York. New York Liberty Zone tax incentives included: (1) an expansion of the work opportunity tax credit (WOTC) for New York Liberty Zone business employees; (2) a special depreciation allowance for qualified New York Liberty Zone property; (3) a five-year recovery period for depreciation of qualified New York Liberty Zone leasehold improvement property; (4) $8 billion of tax-exempt private activity bond financing for certain nonresidential real property, residential rental property and public utility property; (5) $9 billion of additional tax-exempt, advance refunding bonds; (6) increased section 179 expensing; and (7) an extension of the replacement period for nonrecognition of gain for certain involuntary conversions.[3]

The expanded WOTC credit provided a 40 percent subsidy on the first $6,000 of annual wages paid to New York Liberty Zone business employees for work performed during 2002 or 2003.

The special depreciation allowance for qualified New York Liberty Zone property equals 30 percent of the adjusted basis of the property for the taxable year in which the property is placed in service. Qualified nonresidential real property and residential rental property must be purchased by the taxpayer after September 10, 2001, and placed in service before January 1, 2010. Such property is qualified property only to the extent it rehabilitates real property damaged, or replaces real property destroyed or condemned, as a result of the September 11, 2001, terrorist attacks. The provision is no longer applicable for other property.

The five-year recovery period for qualified leasehold improvement property applied, in general, to buildings located in the New York Liberty Zone if the improvement was placed in service after September 10, 2001, and before January 1, 2007, and no written binding contract for the improvement was in effect before September 11, 2001.

The $8 billion of tax-exempt private activity bond financing is authorized to be issued by the State of New York or any political subdivision thereof after March 9, 2002, and before January 1, 2010.

The $9 billion of additional tax-exempt, advance refunding bonds was available after March 9, 2002, and before January 1, 2006, with respect to certain State or local bonds outstanding on September 11, 2001.

---

[3] The Working Families Tax Relief Act of 2004 amended certain of the New York Liberty Zone provisions relating to tax-exempt bonds.

Businesses were allowed to expense the cost of certain qualified New York Liberty Zone property placed in service prior to 2007, up to an additional $35,000 above the amounts generally available under section 179.[4] In addition, only 50 percent of the cost of such qualified New York Liberty Zone property counted toward the limitation under which section 179 deductions are reduced to the extent the cost of section 179 property exceeds a specified amount.

A taxpayer may elect not to recognize gain with respect to property that is involuntarily converted if the taxpayer acquires within an applicable period (the replacement period) property similar or related in service or use. In general, the replacement period begins with the date of the disposition of the converted property and ends two years (three years if the converted property is real property held for the productive use in a trade or business or for investment) after the close of the first taxable year in which any part of the gain upon conversion is realized. The Act extended the replacement period to five years for property in the New York Liberty Zone that was involuntarily converted as a result of the terrorist attacks on September 11, 2001, if substantially all of the use of the replacement property is in New York City.

**Reasons for Change**

Some of the tax benefits that were provided to New York following the attacks of September 11, 2001, likely will not be usable in the form in which they were originally provided. State and local officials in New York have concluded that improvements to transportation infrastructure and connectivity in the Liberty Zone would have a greater impact on recovery and continued development than would some of the existing tax incentive provisions.

**Proposal**

The proposal would sunset certain existing New York Liberty Zone tax benefits and provide in their place tax credits to New York State and New York City for expenditures relating to the construction or improvement of transportation infrastructure in or connecting to the New York Liberty Zone. New York State and New York City each would be eligible for a tax credit for expenditures relating to the construction or improvement of transportation infrastructure in or connecting to the New York Liberty Zone. The tax credit would be allowed in each year from 2010 to 2019, inclusive, subject to an annual limit of $200 million (for a total of $2 billion in tax credits), and would be divided evenly between the State and the City. Any unused credits below the annual limit would be added to the $200 million annual limit for the following year, including years after 2019. Similarly, expenditures that exceed the annual limit would be carried forward and subtracted from the annual limit in the following year. The credit would be allowed against any payments (other than payments of excise taxes and social security and Medicare payroll taxes) made by the City and State under any provision of the Code, including income tax withholding. The Treasury Department would prescribe such rules as are necessary to ensure that

---

[4] Section 179 provides that, in place of depreciation, certain taxpayers, typically small businesses, may elect to deduct up to $125,000 of the cost of section 179 property placed in service each year. In general, section 179 property is defined as depreciable tangible personal property that is purchased for use in the active conduct of a trade or business.

the expenditures are made for the intended purposes. The amount of the credit received would be considered State and local funds for the purpose of any Federal program.

**Repeal Certain New York City Liberty Zone Incentives**

The special depreciation allowance for qualified New York Liberty Zone property that is either nonresidential real property or residential rental property would be terminated as of the date of enactment. Property placed in service after the date of enactment would be ineligible for this incentive unless a binding written contract is in effect on the date of enactment and the property is placed in service before the original sunset dates set forth in the Act.

**Levy Payments to Federal Contractors with Delinquent Tax Debt**

**IMPROVE DEBT COLLECTION ADMINSTRATIVE PROCEDURES**

## Current Law

Before the IRS can issue a levy for an unpaid federal tax liability, it must give the taxpayer an opportunity for an administrative collection due process (CDP) hearing. As exceptions to this general rule, a CDP hearing is not required prior to the IRS issuing a levy for liabilities that arise from either a state tax refund or federal employment taxes. When these exceptions apply, the CDP hearing takes place within a reasonable time after the levy.

Prior to making a disbursement to federal contractors, an automated check for federal tax liabilities generally occurs using the Federal Payment Levy Program (FPLP). When a tax liability is identified, the IRS issues a CDP notice to the federal contractor, but cannot levy the payment until the CDP requirements are complete.

## Reason for Change

When the FPLP identifies a federal contractor as having federal tax liabilities, the opportunity to levy payments to the contractor may be lost because the CDP requirements cannot be completed before the payment is made.

## Proposal

The proposal would allow the IRS to issue levies prior to a CDP hearing for federal tax liabilities of federal contractors identified under the FPLP. When a levy is issued prior to a CDP hearing under this proposal, the taxpayer would have an opportunity for a CDP hearing within a reasonable time after the levy.

The proposal would be effective for levies issued after December 31, 2009.

## INCREASE LEVY AUTHORITY TO 100 PERCENT FOR VENDOR PAYMENTS

### Current Law

If a federal vendor has an unpaid tax liability, the IRS can levy 100 percent of any payment due to the vendor for goods or services sold or leased to the federal government.

### Reason for Change

The statutory language "goods or services sold or leased" has been interpreted as excluding payments for the sale or lease of real estate or other types of property not considered "goods or services."

### Proposal

The proposal would clarify that the IRS can levy 100 percent of any payment due to a federal vendor with unpaid tax liabilities, including payments made for the sale or lease of real estate and other types of property not considered "goods or services."

The proposal would be effective for payments made after the proposal's date of enactment.

**REVENUES DEDICATED TO THE HEALTH REFORM RESERVE FUND**

**LIMIT THE TAX RATE AT WHICH ITEMIZED DEDUCTIONS REDUCE TAX LIABILITY TO 28 PERCENT**

## Current Law

Current law permits the allowable portion of an individual taxpayer's itemized deductions to reduce the amount of taxable income. This, in effect, applies those deductions first to the taxable income in the highest tax bracket, and then to the next lower tax brackets in descending order.

Individual taxpayers may elect to itemize their deductions instead of claiming a standard deduction. In general, itemized deductions include medical and dental expenses (in excess of 7.5 percent of AGI), state and local property taxes and either income or sales taxes, interest paid, gifts to charities, casualty and theft losses (in excess of 10 percent of AGI), and job expenses and certain miscellaneous expenses (some only in excess of 2 percent of AGI).

For higher-income taxpayers, otherwise allowable itemized deductions (other than medical expenses, investment interest, theft and casualty losses, and gambling losses) are reduced if AGI exceeds a statutory floor that is indexed annually for inflation. Prior to the enactment of EGTRRA, itemized deductions were reduced by 3 percent of AGI over the threshold but not by more than 80 percent of the otherwise allowable deductions. EGTRRA reduced the itemized deduction limitation in three steps. For 2006 and 2007, itemized deductions were reduced by 2 percent of AGI over the threshold, but not by more than 53-1/3 percent. For 2008 and 2009, itemized deductions were reduced by 1 percent of AGI over the threshold, but not by more than 26-2/3 percent. For 2010, the reduction was to be completely eliminated. However, beginning in 2011, the full itemized deduction reduction of 3 percent of AGI exceeding the floor, but not by more than 80 percent, is scheduled to be reinstated.

For 2009, the AGI floor is $166,800 ($83,400 if married filing separately).

A separate Budget proposal would adjust the 2011 income thresholds beyond which itemized deductions are reduced to $250,000 (indexed for inflation from 2009) for married taxpayers filing jointly and $200,000 (indexed from 2009) for single taxpayers. Thereafter, the thresholds would be indexed for inflation annually.

## Reason for Change

Many itemized deductions reflect social policies of encouraging taxpayers to engage in certain activities by reducing the after-tax cost of those activities. Many worthwhile activities compete for the resources that are available. The Administration believes that limiting the benefits from certain itemized deductions to not more than 28 percent of the taxpayer's outlays would provide some of the resources necessary to fund important reforms to the medical care and medical insurance systems.

## Proposal

The proposal would limit the value of all itemized deductions by limiting the tax value of those deductions to 28 percent whenever they would otherwise reduce taxable income in the 36 or 39.6 percent tax brackets. A similar limitation also would apply under the AMT.

This proposal would apply to itemized deductions after they have been reduced under a separate budget proposal that would reinstate the pre-EGTRRA limitation on certain itemized deductions, but with adjusted AGI thresholds in 2011 of $250,000 (indexed from 2009) for married taxpayers filing jointly and $200,000 (indexed from 2009) for other taxpayers. After 2011, these thresholds would be indexed.

The proposal is effective for taxable years beginning after December 31, 2010.

## REDUCE THE TAX GAP AND MAKE REFORMS

### Expand Information Reporting

## REQUIRE INFORMATION REPORTING FOR PRIVATE SEPARATE ACCOUNTS OF LIFE INSURANCE COMPANIES

### Current Law

Earnings from direct investment in securities generally result in taxable income to the holder. In contrast, investments in comparable assets through a separate account of a life insurance company generally give rise to tax-free or tax-deferred income. This favorable tax treatment for investing through a life insurance company is not available if the policyholder has so much control over the investments in the separate account that the policyholder, rather than the insurance company, is treated as the owner of those investments.

### Reasons for Change

In some cases, private separate accounts are being used to avoid tax that would be due if the assets were held directly. Better reporting of investments in private separate accounts will help the IRS to ensure that income is properly reported. Moreover, such reporting will enable the IRS to identify more easily which variable insurance contracts qualify as insurance contracts under current law and which contracts should be disregarded under the investor control doctrine.

### Proposal

The proposal would require life insurance companies to report to the IRS, for each contract whose cash value is partially or wholly invested in a private separate account for any portion of the taxable year, the policyholder's taxpayer identification number, the policy number, the amount of accumulated untaxed income, the total contract account value, and the portion of that value that was invested in one or more private separate accounts. For this purpose, a private separate account would be defined as any account with respect to which a related group of persons owned policies whose cash values, in the aggregate, represented at least 10 percent of the value of the separate account.

The proposal would be effective for taxable years beginning after December 31, 2010.

# REQUIRE INFORMATION REPORTING ON PAYMENTS TO CORPORATIONS

## Current Law

Generally, a taxpayer making payments to a recipient aggregating to $600 or more for services or determinable gains in the course of a trade or business in a calendar year is required to send an information return to the IRS setting forth the amount, as well as name and address of the recipient of the payment (generally on Form 1099). Under a longstanding regulatory regime, there are certain exceptions for payments to corporations, as well as tax-exempt and government entities.

## Reasons for Change

Generally, compliance increases significantly for payments that a third party reports to the IRS. In the case of tax-exempt or government entities that are generally not subject to income tax, information returns may not be necessary. On the other hand, during the decades in which the regulatory exception for payments to corporations has become established, the number and complexity of corporate taxpayers have increased. Moreover, the longstanding regulatory exception from information reporting for payments to corporations has created compliance issues. Although the exception for information reporting to corporations is set forth in existing regulations, because it has been in place for many years and because Congress, during that time period, has made numerous changes to the information reporting rules, elimination of the exception should be made by legislative change.

## Proposal

A business would be required to file an information return for payments aggregating to $600 or more in a calendar year to a corporation (except a tax-exempt corporation).

The proposal would be effective for payments made to corporations after December 31, 2009.

## REQUIRE A CERTIFIED TAXPAYER IDENTIFICATION NUMBER FROM CONTRACTORS AND ALLOW CERTAIN WITHHOLDING

### Current Law

In the course of a trade or business, service recipients ("businesses") making payments aggregating to $600 or more in a calendar year to any non-employee service provider ("contractor") that is not a corporation are required to send an information return to the IRS setting forth the amount, as well as name, address, and taxpayer identification number (TIN) of the contractor. The information returns, required annually after the end of the year, are made on Form 1099-MISC based on identifying information furnished by the contractor but not verified by the IRS. Copies are provided both to the contractor and to the IRS. Withholding is not required or permitted for payments to contractors. Since contractors are not subject to withholding, they may be required to make quarterly payments of estimated income taxes and self-employment (SECA) taxes near the end of each calendar quarter. The contractor is required to pay any balance due when the annual income tax return is subsequently filed.

### Reasons for Change

Without accurate taxpayer identifying information, information reporting requirements impose avoidable burdens on businesses and the IRS, and cannot reach their potential to improve compliance.

Estimated tax filing is relatively burdensome, especially for less sophisticated and lower-income taxpayers. Moreover, by the time estimated tax payments (or final tax payments) are due, some contractors will not have put aside the necessary funds. Given that the SECA tax rate is 15.3 percent (up to certain income limits), the required tax payments can be more than 25 percent of a contractor's gross receipts, even for a contractor with modest income.

An optional withholding method for contractors would reduce the burdens of having to make quarterly payments, would help contractors automatically set aside funds for tax payments, and would help increase compliance.

### Proposal

A contractor receiving payments of $600 or more in a calendar year from a particular business would be required to furnish to the business (on Form W-9) the contractor's certified TIN. A business would be required to verify the contractor's TIN with the IRS, which would be authorized to disclose, solely for this purpose, whether the certified TIN-name combination matches IRS records. If a contractor failed to furnish an accurate certified TIN, the business would be required to withhold a flat-rate percentage of gross payments. Contractors receiving payments of $600 or more in a calendar year from a particular business could require the business to withhold a flat-rate percentage of their gross payments, with the flat-rate percentage of 15, 25, 30, or 35 percent being selected by the contractor.

The proposal would be effective for payments made to contractors after December 31, 2009.

# REQUIRE INCREASED INFORMATION REPORTING FOR CERTAIN GOVERNMENT PAYMENTS FOR PROPERTY AND SERVICES

## Current Law

Businesses, governments, and other taxpayers are subject to a number of information reporting and withholding requirements. Generally, a taxpayer making payments aggregating to $600 or more for services or determinable gains in the course of a trade or business in a calendar year is required to send an information return to the IRS (except if the recipient is a corporation) setting forth the amount, as well as the name and address of the recipient of the payment (generally on Form 1099). In addition, any service recipient engaged in a trade or business is required to file an information return if the aggregate of payments for services is $600 or more in a calendar year. This requirement specifically applies to government agencies, even if the service provider is a corporation. Moreover, Federal agencies must file information returns with respect to contractors, generally on Form 8596 (Information Return for Federal Contracts) and Form 8596A (Quarterly Transmittal of Information Returns for Federal Contracts). Under recently enacted legislation that will take effect in 2012, Federal, State and local government agencies generally must withhold 3 percent of payments for goods or services. Exceptions apply to certain payments such as those actually subjected to backup withholding, wages and public assistance.

## Reasons for Change

Generally, compliance increases significantly for payments that a third party reports to the IRS. Some government vendors fail to meet their tax filing and payment obligations.

## Proposal

The IRS and Treasury Department would be authorized to promulgate regulations requiring information reporting on all non-wage payments by Federal, State and local governments to procure property or services. It is expected that certain categories of payments would be excluded from the new information reporting requirements, including payments of interest, payments for real property, payments to tax-exempt entities or foreign governments, intergovernmental payments, and payments made pursuant to a classified or confidential contract.

The proposal would be effective for payments made after December 31, 2009.

# INCREASE INFORMATION RETURN PENALTIES

## Current Law

There are a number of information reporting requirements under the Code. When these requirements are not followed, penalties may apply based on whether and when a correct information return is filed. If a person subject to the information reporting requirements files a correct information return after the prescribed filing date, but on or before the date that is thirty days after the prescribed filing date, the amount of the penalty is $15 per return (the "first-tier penalty"), not to exceed $75,000 per calendar year. If such a person files a correct information return more than thirty days after the prescribed filing date but on or before August 1, the amount of the penalty is $30 per return (the "second-tier penalty"), not to exceed $150,000 per calendar year. If such a person does not file a correct information return on or before August 1, the amount of the penalty is $50 per return (the "third-tier penalty"), not to exceed $250,000 in a calendar year. For certain small filers whose average annual gross receipts do not exceed $5,000,000, the maximum calendar year limit is $25,000 (instead of $75,000) for the first-tier penalty, $50,000 (instead of $150,000) for the second-tier penalty, and $100,000 (instead of $250,000) for the third-tier penalty. If a failure is due to intentional disregard of a filing requirement, the minimum penalty for each failure is $100, with no calendar year limit.

## Reasons for Change

Generally, compliance increases significantly with respect to amounts reported on information returns. In some cases, filers may have failed to comply with existing information reporting requirements because the amount of the potentially applicable penalties is too small to discourage non-compliance. Increasing the penalty amounts, which were established in 1989 and have not been increased, will help to ensure the timely filing of accurate information returns.

## Proposal

The first-tier penalty would be increased from $15 to $30, and the calendar year maximum would be increased from $75,000 to $250,000. The second-tier penalty would be increased from $30 to $60, and the calendar year maximum would be increased from $150,000 to $500,000. The third-tier penalty would be increased from $50 to $100, and the calendar year maximum would be increased from $250,000 to $1,500,000. For small filers, the calendar year maximum would be increased from $25,000 to $75,000 for the first-tier penalty, from $50,000 to $200,000 for the second-tier penalty, and from $100,000 to $500,000 for the third-tier penalty. The minimum penalty for each failure due to intentional disregard would be increased from $100 to $250. The proposal would also provide that every five years the penalty amounts would be adjusted to account for inflation.

The proposal would be effective for information returns required to be filed after December 31, 2010.

**Improve Compliance by Business**

## REQUIRE E-FILING BY CERTAIN LARGE ORGANIZATIONS

### Current Law

Effective for tax years ending on or after December 31, 2005, corporations with assets of $10 million or more filing Form 1120 are required to file Schedule M-3 (Net Income (Loss) Reconciliation for Corporations with Total Assets of $10 Million or More). Effective for tax years ending on or after December 31, 2006, this Schedule M-3 filing requirement also applies to S corporations, life insurance corporations, property and casualty insurance corporations, and cooperative associations filing various versions of Form 1120 and having $10 million or more in assets. Schedule M-3 is also required for partnerships with assets of $10 million or more and certain other partnerships.

Corporations and tax-exempt organizations that have assets of $10 million or more and file at least 250 returns during a calendar year, including income tax, information, excise tax, and employment tax returns, are required to file electronically their Form 1120/1120S income tax returns and Form 990 information returns for tax years ending on or after December 31, 2006. In addition, private foundations and charitable trusts that file at least 250 returns during a calendar year are required to file electronically their Form 990-PF information returns for tax years ending on or after December 31, 2006, regardless of their asset size. Taxpayers can request waivers of the electronic filing requirement if they cannot meet that requirement due to technological constraints, or if compliance with the requirement would result in undue financial burden on the taxpayer. Although electronic filing is required of certain corporations and other taxpayers, others may convert voluntarily to electronic filing.

Generally, regulations may require electronic filing by taxpayers (other than individuals, estates and trusts) that file at least 250 returns annually. Before requiring electronic filing, the IRS and Treasury Department must take into account the ability of taxpayers to comply at a reasonable cost.

### Reasons for Change

Generally, compliance increases when taxpayers are required to provide better information to the IRS in usable form. Large organizations with assets of $10 million or more generally maintain financial records in electronic form, and generally either hire tax professionals who use tax preparation software or use tax preparation software themselves although they may not currently file electronically.

Electronic filing supports the broader goals of improving IRS service to taxpayers, enhancing compliance, and modernizing tax administration. Overall, increased electronic filing of returns may improve customer satisfaction and confidence in the filing process, and it may be more cost effective for affected entities. Expanding electronic filing to certain additional large entities will help provide tax return information in a more uniform electronic form. This will enhance the ability of the IRS to more productively focus its audit activities. This can reduce burdens on businesses where the need for an audit can be avoided.

In the case of a large business, adopting the same standard for electronic filing as for filing Schedule M-3 provides simplification benefits.

## **Proposal**

All corporations and partnerships required to file Schedule M-3 would be required to file their tax returns electronically. In the case of certain other large taxpayers not required to file Schedule M-3 (such as exempt organizations), the regulatory authority to require electronic filing would be expanded to allow reduction of the current threshold of filing 250 or more returns during a calendar year. Nevertheless, any new regulations would balance the benefits of electronic filing against any burden that might be imposed on taxpayers, and implementation would take place incrementally to afford adequate time for transition to electronic filing. Taxpayers would be able to request waivers of this requirement if they cannot meet the requirement due to technological constraints, if compliance with the requirement would result in undue financial burden, or if other criteria specified in regulations are met.

The proposal would be effective for tax years ending after December 31, 2009.

**IMPLEMENT STANDARDS CLARIFYING WHEN EMPLOYEE LEASING COMPANIES CAN BE HELD LIABLE FOR THEIR CLIENTS' FEDERAL EMPLOYMENT TAXES**

## Current Law

Employers are required to withhold and pay Federal Insurance Contribution Act (FICA) and income taxes, and are required to pay Federal Unemployment Tax Act (FUTA) taxes (collectively "Federal employment taxes") with respect to wages paid to their employees. Liability for Federal employment taxes generally lies with the taxpayer that is determined to be the employer under a multi-factor common law test or under specific statutory provisions. For example, a third party that is not the common law employer can be a statutory employer if the third party has control over the payment of wages. In addition, certain designated agents are jointly and severally liable with their principals for employment taxes with respect to wages paid to the principals' employees. These designated agents prepare and file employment tax returns using their own name and employer identification number. In contrast, reporting agents (often referred to as payroll service providers) are generally not liable for the employment taxes reported on their clients' returns. Reporting agents prepare and file employment tax returns for their clients using the client's name and employer identification number.

Employee leasing is the practice of contracting with an outside business to handle certain administrative, personnel, and payroll matters for a taxpayer's employees. Employee leasing companies (often referred to as professional employer organizations) typically prepare and file employment tax returns for their clients using the leasing company's name and employer identification number, often taking the position that the leasing company is the statutory or common law employer of their clients' workers.

## Reasons for Change

Under present law, there is often uncertainty as to whether the employee leasing company or its client is liable for unpaid Federal employment taxes arising with respect to wages paid to the client's workers. Thus, when an employee leasing company files employment tax returns using its own name and employer identification number, but fails to pay some or all of the taxes due, or when no returns are filed with respect to wages paid by a taxpayer that uses an employee leasing company, there can be uncertainty as to how the Federal employment taxes are assessed and collected.

Providing standards for when an employee leasing company and its clients will be held liable for Federal employment taxes will facilitate the assessment, payment and collection of those taxes and will preclude taxpayers who have control over withholding and payment of those taxes from denying liability when the taxes are not paid.

## Proposal

The proposal would set forth standards for holding employee leasing companies jointly and severally liable with their clients for Federal employment taxes. The proposal would also provide standards for holding employee leasing companies solely liable for such taxes if they meet specified requirements.

The provision would be effective for employment tax returns required to be filed with respect to wages paid after December 31, 2009.

**Strengthen Tax Administration**

## ALLOW ASSESSMENT OF CRIMINAL RESTITUTION AS TAX

### Current Law

In criminal tax cases, a District Court may issue an order requiring the defendant to pay restitution of existing tax liabilities. The District Court has authority to order restitution under the criminal provisions of Title 18, not the Internal Revenue Code (Code). Because the assessment procedures under the Code apply only to taxes imposed by the Code, those procedures do not apply to restitution orders issued under Title 18, even if the restitution order relates to an existing tax liability.

### Reasons for Change

Because court-ordered restitution in criminal tax cases cannot be assessed as a tax, the IRS cannot use its existing assessment systems to collect and enforce the restitution obligation. This leads to unnecessary duplication of efforts, delays, and confusion in the administration of court-ordered restitution.

### Proposal

The proposal would allow the IRS and the Treasury Department to immediately assess, without issuing a statutory notice of deficiency, and collect as a tax debt court-ordered restitution. The taxpayer would not be able to collaterally attack the amount of restitution ordered by the court, but would retain the ability to challenge the method of collection.

The proposal would be effective after December 31, 2010.

## REVISE OFFER-IN-COMPROMISE APPLICATION RULES

### Current Law

Current law provides that the IRS may compromise any civil or criminal case arising under the internal revenue laws prior to a reference to the Department of Justice for prosecution or defense. In 2006, a new provision was enacted to require taxpayers to make certain nonrefundable payments with any initial offer-in-compromise of a tax case. The new provision requires taxpayers making a lump-sum offer-in-compromise to include a nonrefundable payment of 20 percent of the lump-sum with the initial offer. In the case of an offer-in-compromise involving periodic payments, the initial offer must be accompanied by a nonrefundable payment of the first installment that would be due if the offer were accepted.

### Reasons for Change

Requiring nonrefundable payments with an offer-in-compromise may substantially reduce access to the offer-in-compromise program. The offer-in-compromise program is designed to settle cases in which taxpayers have demonstrated an inability to pay the full amount of a tax liability. The program allows the IRS to collect the portion of a tax liability that the taxpayer has the ability to pay. Reducing access to the offer-in-compromise program makes it more difficult and costly to obtain the collectable portion of existing tax liabilities.

### Proposal

The proposal would eliminate the requirements that an initial offer-in-compromise include a nonrefundable payment of any portion of the taxpayer's offer.

The proposal would be for offers-in-compromise submitted after the date of enactment.

**EXPAND IRS ACCESS TO INFORMATION IN THE NATIONAL DIRECTORY OF NEW HIRES FOR TAX ADMINISTRATION PURPOSES**

## Current Law

The Office of Child Support Enforcement of the Department of Health and Human Services (HHS) maintains the National Directory of New Hires (NDNH), which is a database that contains newly-hired employee data from Form W-4, quarterly wage data from State and Federal employment security agencies, and unemployment benefit data from State unemployment insurance agencies. The NDNH was created to help State child support enforcement agencies enforce obligations of parents across State lines.

Under current provisions of the Social Security Act, the IRS may obtain data from the NDNH, but only for the purpose of administering the EITC and verifying employment reported on a tax return.

Generally, the IRS obtains employment and unemployment data less frequently than quarterly, and there are significant internal costs of preparing these data for use. Under various State laws, the IRS may negotiate for access to employment and unemployment data directly from State agencies that maintain these data.

## Reasons for Change

Employment data are useful to the IRS in administering a wide range of tax provisions beyond the EITC, including verifying taxpayer claims and identifying levy sources. Currently, the IRS may obtain employment and unemployment data on a State-by-State basis, which is a costly and time-consuming process. NDNH data are timely, uniformly compiled, and electronically accessible. Access to the NDNH would increase the productivity of the IRS by reducing the amount of IRS resources dedicated to obtaining and processing data without reducing the current levels of taxpayer privacy.

## Proposal

The Social Security Act would be amended to expand IRS access to NDNH data for general tax administration purposes, including data matching, verification of taxpayer claims during return processing, preparation of substitute returns for non-compliant taxpayers, and identification of levy sources. Data obtained by the IRS from the NDNH would be protected by existing taxpayer privacy law, including civil and criminal sanctions.

The proposal would be effective upon enactment.

# MAKE REPEATED WILLFUL FAILURE TO FILE A TAX RETURN A FELONY

## Current Law

Current law provides that willful failure to file a tax return is a misdemeanor punishable by a term of imprisonment for not more than one year, a fine of not more than $25,000 ($100,000 in the case of a corporation), or both. A taxpayer who fails to file returns for multiple years commits a separate misdemeanor offense for each year.

## Reasons for Change

Increased criminal penalties would help to deter multiple willful failures to file tax returns.

## Proposal

Any person who willfully fails to file tax returns in any three years within any five consecutive year period, if the aggregated tax liability for such period is at least $50,000, would be subject to a new aggravated failure to file criminal penalty. The proposal would classify such failure as a felony and, upon conviction, impose a fine of not more than $250,000 ($500,000 in the case of a corporation) or imprisonment for not more than five years, or both.

The proposal would be effective for returns required to be filed after December 31, 2009.

# FACILITATE TAX COMPLIANCE WITH LOCAL JURISDICTIONS

## Current Law

Although Federal tax returns and return information (FTI) generally are confidential, the IRS and Treasury Department may share FTI with States as well as certain local government entities that are treated as States for this purpose. Generally, the purpose of information sharing is to facilitate tax administration. Where sharing of FTI is authorized, reciprocal provisions generally authorize disclosure of information to the IRS by State and local governments. State and local governments that receive FTI must safeguard it according to prescribed protocols that require secure storage, restricted access, reports to IRS, and shredding or other proper disposal. See, e.g., IRS Publication 1075. Criminal and civil sanctions apply to unauthorized disclosure or inspection of FTI. Indian Tribal Governments (ITGs) are treated as States by the tax law for several purposes, such as certain charitable contributions, excise tax credits, and local tax deductions, but not for purposes of information sharing.

## Reasons for Change

IRS and Treasury compliance activity, especially with respect to alcohol, tobacco and fuel excise taxes, may necessitate information sharing with ITGs. For example, the IRS may wish to confirm if a fuel supplier's claim to have delivered particular amounts to adjacent jurisdictions is consistent with that reported to the IRS. If not, the IRS in conjunction with the ITG, which would have responsibility for administering taxes imposed by the ITG, can take steps to ensure compliance with both Federal and ITG tax laws. Where the local government is treated as a State for information sharing purposes, IRS, Treasury, and local officials can support each other's efforts. Where the local government is not so treated, there is an impediment to compliance activity.

## Proposal

ITGs that impose alcohol, tobacco, or fuel excise or income or wage taxes would be treated as States for purposes of information sharing to the extent necessary for ITG tax administration. An ITG that receives FTI would be required to safeguard it according to prescribed protocols. The criminal and civil sanctions would apply.

The proposal would be effective for disclosures made after enactment.

## EXTENSION OF STATUTE OF LIMITATIONS WHERE STATE TAX ADJUSTMENT AFFECTS FEDERAL TAX LIABILITY

### Current Law

In general, additional Federal tax liabilities in the form of tax, interest, penalties and additions to tax must be assessed by the IRS within three years after the date a return is filed. If an assessment is not made within the required time period, the additional liabilities generally cannot be assessed or collected at any future time. The Code contains exceptions to the general statute of limitations. In general, the statute of limitations with respect to claims for refund expires three years from the time the return was filed or two years from the time the tax was paid, whichever is later.

State and local authorities employ a variety of statutes of limitations for State and local tax assessments. Pursuant to agreement, the IRS and State and local revenue agencies exchange reports of adjustments made through examination so that corresponding adjustments can be made by each taxing authority. In addition, States provide the IRS with reports of potential discrepancies between State returns and Federal returns.

### Reasons for Change

The general statute of limitations serves as a barrier to the effective use by the IRS of State and local tax adjustment reports when the reports are provided by the State or local revenue agency to the IRS with little time remaining for assessments to be made at the Federal level. Under the current statute of limitations framework, taxpayers may seek to extend the State statute of limitations or postpone agreement to State proposed adjustments until such time as the Federal statute of limitations expires in order to preclude assessment at the Federal level. In addition, it is not always the case that a taxpayer that files an amended State or local return reporting additional liabilities at the State or local level that also affect Federal tax liability will file an amended return at the Federal level.

### Proposal

The proposal would create an additional exception to the general three-year statute of limitations for assessment of Federal tax liability resulting from adjustments to State or local tax liability. The statute of limitations would be extended the greater of: (1) one year from the date the taxpayer first files an amended tax return with the IRS reflecting adjustments to the State or local tax return; or (2) two years from the date the IRS first receives information from the State or local revenue agency under an information sharing agreement in place between the IRS and a State or local revenue agency. The statute of limitations would be extended only with respect to the increase in Federal tax attributable to the State or local tax adjustment. The statute of limitations would not be further extended if the taxpayer files additional amended returns for the same tax periods as the initial amended return or if the IRS receives additional information from the State or local revenue agency under an information sharing agreement. The statute of limitations on claims for refund would be extended correspondingly so that any overall increase in tax assessed by the IRS as a result of the State or local examination report would take into account agreed-upon tax decreases or reductions attributable to a refund or credit.

The proposal would be effective for returns required to be filed after December 31, 2009.

# IMPROVE INVESTIGATIVE DISCLOSURE STATUTE

## Current Law

Generally, tax return information is confidential, unless a specific exception in the Code applies. In the case of tax administration, the Code permits Treasury and IRS officers and employees to disclose return information to the extent necessary to obtain information not otherwise reasonably available, in the course of an audit or investigation, as prescribed by regulation. Thus, for example, a revenue agent may identify himself or herself as affiliated with the IRS, and may disclose the nature and subject of an investigation, as necessary to elicit information from a witness in connection with that investigation. Criminal and civil sanctions apply to unauthorized disclosures of return information.

## Reasons for Change

Treasury Regulations effective since 2003 state that the term "necessary" in this context does not mean essential or indispensable, but rather appropriate and helpful in obtaining the information sought. In other contexts, a "necessary" disclosure is one without which performance cannot be accomplished reasonably without the disclosure. Determining if an investigative disclosure is "necessary" is inherently factual, leading to inconsistent opinions by the courts. Eliminating this uncertainty from the statute would facilitate investigations by IRS officers and employees, while setting forth clear guidance for taxpayers, thus enhancing compliance with the tax Code.

## Proposal

The taxpayer privacy law would be clarified by stating that it does not prohibit Treasury and IRS officers and employees from identifying themselves, their organizational affiliation, and the nature and subject of an investigation, when contacting third parties in connection with a civil or criminal tax investigation.

The proposal would be effective for disclosure made after enactment.

# EXPAND REQUIRED ELECTRONIC FILING BY TAX RETURN PREPARERS

## Current Law

The Department of the Treasury currently may issue regulations regarding when tax returns must be filed electronically on magnetic media or in other machine-readable form. But the regulations may not require individuals, estates, or trusts to file their tax returns electronically. In addition, the regulations may not require any person to file electronically unless the person files at least 250 tax returns during the calendar year.

## Reasons for Change

Electronic filing benefits taxpayers and the IRS because it decreases processing errors, expedites processing and payment of tax refunds, and allows the IRS to efficiently maintain up-to-date taxpayer records.

## Proposal

The proposal generally would maintain the current rule that regulations may not require any person to file electronically unless the person files at least 250 tax returns during the calendar year. But the proposal also would provide an exception to this rule under which regulations may require electronic filing by tax return preparers (as currently defined in the Internal Revenue Code) who file more than 100 tax returns in a calendar year. The proposal also would allow regulations requiring tax return preparers who file more than 100 returns (or any other person who files more than 250 returns) to file electronically tax returns for individuals, estates, or trusts.

The proposal would be effective for tax returns required to be filed after December 31, 2010.

**Expand Penalties**

## CLARIFY THAT THE BAD CHECK PENALTY APPLIES TO ELECTRONIC CHECKS AND OTHER PAYMENT FORMS

### Current Law

The Code imposes a penalty on any taxpayer who attempts to satisfy a tax liability with a check or money that is not duly paid. The penalty is 2 percent of the amount of the bad check or money order. If the bad check or money order is for less than $1,250, the penalty is the lesser of $25 or the amount of the check or money order.

### Reasons for Change

Taxpayers use a variety of commercially acceptable instruments to pay tax liabilities, but only two types of instruments are covered by the Code's bad check penalty: checks and money orders.

### Proposal

The proposal would expand the bad check penalty to cover all commercially acceptable instruments of payment that are not duly paid.

The proposal would be effective for returns required to be filed after December 31, 2009.

# IMPOSE PENALTY ON FAILURE TO COMPLY WITH ELECTRONIC FILING REQUIREMENTS

## Current Law

Certain corporations and tax-exempt organizations (including certain charitable trusts and private foundations) are required to file their returns electronically. Generally, filing on paper instead of electronically is treated as a failure to file if electronic filing is required. Additions to tax are imposed for the failure to file tax returns reporting a liability. For failure to file a corporate return, the addition to tax is 5 percent on the amount required to be shown as tax due on the return, for the first month of failure, and an additional 5 percent for each month or part of a month thereafter, up to a maximum of 25 percent.

For failure to file a tax-exempt organization return, the addition to tax is $20 a day for each day the failure continues. The maximum amount per return is $10,000 or 5 percent of the organization's gross receipts for the year, whichever is less. Organizations with annual gross receipts exceeding $1 million, however, are subject to an addition to tax of $100 per day, with a maximum of $50,000.

## Reasons for Change

Although there are additions to tax for the failure to file returns, there is no specific penalty in the tax Code for a failure to comply with a requirement to file electronically. Because the addition to tax for failure to file a corporate return is based on an underpayment of tax, no addition is imposed if the corporation is in a refund, credit, or loss status. Thus, the existing addition to tax may not provide an adequate incentive for certain corporations to file electronically. Generally, electronic filing increases efficiency of tax administration because the provision of tax return information in an electronic form enables the IRS to focus audit activities where they can have the greatest impact. This also assists taxpayers where the need for audit is reduced.

## Proposal

The proposal would establish an assessable penalty would be established for a failure to comply with a requirement of electronic (or other machine-readable) format for a return that is filed. The amount of the penalty would be $25,000 for a corporation or $5,000 for a tax-exempt organization. For failure to file in any format, the existing penalty would remain, and the proposed penalty would not apply.

The proposal would be effective for returns required to be electronically filed after December 31, 2010.

# MAKE REFORMS TO CLOSE TAX LOOPHOLES

## Financial Institutions and Products

## REQUIRE ACCRUAL OF INCOME ON FORWARD SALE OF CORPORATE STOCK

### Current Law

A corporation generally does not recognize gain or loss on the issuance or repurchase of its own stock. Thus, a corporation does not recognize gain or loss on the forward sale of its own stock. A corporation sells its stock forward by agreeing to issue its stock in the future in exchange for consideration to be paid in the future.

Although a corporation does not recognize gain or loss on the issuance of its own stock, a corporation does recognize interest income upon the current sale of stock for deferred payment.

### Reasons for Change

There is little substantive difference between a corporate issuer's current sale of its stock for deferred payment and an issuer's forward sale of the same stock. The only difference between the two transactions is the timing of the stock issuance. In a current sale, the stock is issued at the inception of the transaction, while, in a forward sale, the stock is issued at the time the deferred payment is received. In both cases, a portion of the deferred payment economically compensates the corporation for the time-value of the deferred payment. It is inappropriate to treat these two transactions differently.

### Proposal

The proposal would require a corporation that enters into a forward contract to issue its stock to treat a portion of the payment on the forward issuance as a payment of interest.

The proposal would be effective for forward contracts entered into after December 31, 2010.

# REQUIRE ORDINARY TREATMENT FOR CERTAIN DEALERS OF EQUITY OPTIONS AND COMMODITIES

## Current Law

Under current law, commodities dealers (within the meaning of section 1402(i)(2)(B)), commodities derivatives dealers (within the meaning of section 1221(b)(1)(A)), dealers in securities (within the meaning of section 475(c)(1)) and options dealers (within the meaning of section 1256(g)(8)), treat the income from certain of their day-to-day dealer activities as giving rise to capital gain. Under section 1256, these dealers treat 60 percent of their income (or loss) from their dealer activities as long-term capital gain (or loss) and 40 percent of their income (or loss) from their dealer activities as short-term capital gain (or loss). Dealers in other types of property generally treat the income from their day-to-day dealer activities as giving rise to ordinary income.

## Reasons for Change

There is no reason to treat dealers in commodities, commodities derivatives dealers, dealers in securities and dealers in equity options differently than dealers in other types of property. Dealers earn their income from their day-to-day dealing activities and should be taxed at ordinary rates.

## Proposal

The proposal would require commodities derivatives dealers, dealers in securities and dealers in equity options and commodities and to treat the income from their day-to-day dealer activities as ordinary in character, not capital.

The proposal would be effective for taxable years beginning after the date of enactment.

## MODIFY DEFINITION OF CONTROL FOR PURPOSES OF THE SECTION 249 DEDUCTION LIMIT

### Current Law

In general, if a corporation repurchases a debt instrument that is convertible into its stock, or into stock of a corporation in control of or controlled by the corporation, section 249 may disallow or limit the issuer's deduction for a premium paid to repurchase the debt instrument. For this purpose, "control" is determined by reference to section 368(c), which encompasses only direct relationships (e.g., a parent corporation and its wholly-owned, first tier subsidiary).

### Reasons for Change

The definition of "control" in section 249 is unnecessarily restrictive, and has resulted in situations in which the limitation in section 249 is too easily avoided. Indirect control relationships (e.g., a parent corporation and a second-tier subsidiary) present the same economic identity of interests as direct control relationships, and should be treated in a similar manner.

### Proposal

Under the proposal, the definition of "control" in section 249(b)(2) would be amended to incorporate indirect control relationships, of the nature described in section 1563(a)(1).

The proposal would be effective on the date of enactment.

**Insurance Companies and Products**

## MODIFY RULES THAT APPLY TO SALES OF LIFE INSURANCE CONTRACTS

### Current Law

The seller of a life insurance contract generally must report as taxable income the difference between the amount received from the buyer and the adjusted basis in the contract, unless the buyer is a viatical settlement provider and the insured person is terminally or chronically ill.

Under a transfer-for-value rule, the buyer of a previously-issued life insurance contract who subsequently receives a death benefit generally is subject to tax on the difference between the death benefit received and the sum of the amount paid for the contract and premiums subsequently paid by the buyer. This rule does not apply if the buyer's basis is determined in whole or in part by reference to the seller's basis, nor does the rule apply if the buyer is the insured, a partner of the insured, a partnership in which the insured is a partner, or a corporation in which the insured is a shareholder or officer.

Persons engaged in a trade or business that make payments of premiums, compensations, remunerations, other fixed or determinable gains, profits and income, or certain other types of payments in the course of that trade or business to another person generally are required to report such payments of $600 or more to the IRS. However, reporting may not be required in some circumstances involving the purchase of a life insurance contract.

### Reasons for Change

Recent years have seen a significant increase in the number and size of life settlement transactions, wherein individuals sell previously-issued life insurance contracts to investors. Compliance is sometimes hampered by a lack of information reporting. In addition, the current law exceptions to the transfer-for-value rule may give investors the ability to structure a transaction to avoid paying tax on the profit when the insured person dies.

### Proposal

The proposal would require a person or entity who purchases an interest in an existing life insurance contract with a death benefit equal to or exceeding $1 million to report the purchase price, the buyer's and seller's taxpayer identification numbers (TINs), and the issuer and policy number to the IRS, to the insurance company that issued the policy, and to the seller.

The proposal also would modify the transfer-for-value rule to ensure that exceptions to that rule would not apply to buyers of policies. Upon the payment of any policy benefits to the buyer, the insurance company would be required to report the gross benefit payment, the buyer's TIN, and the insurance company's estimate of the buyer's basis to the IRS and to the payee.

The proposal would apply to sales or assignment of interests in life insurance policies and payments of death benefits for taxable years beginning after December 31, 2010.

## MODIFY DIVIDENDS-RECEIVED DEDUCTION FOR LIFE INSURANCE COMPANY SEPARATE ACCOUNTS

### Current Law

Corporate taxpayers may generally qualify for a dividends-received deduction (DRD) with regard to dividends received from other domestic corporations, in order to prevent or limit taxable inclusion of the same income by more than one corporation. In the case of a life insurance company, the DRD is permitted only with regard to the "company's share" of dividends received, reflecting the fact that some portion of the company's dividend income is used to fund tax-deductible reserves for its obligations to policyholders. Likewise, the net increase or net decrease in reserves is computed by reducing the ending balance of the reserve items by the policyholders' share of tax-exempt interest. The regime for computing the company's share and policyholders' share of net investment income is sometimes referred to as proration.

A life insurance company's separate account assets, liabilities, and income are segregated from those of the company's general account in order to support variable life insurance and variable annuity contracts. A company's share and policyholders' share are computed for the company's general account and separately for each separate account.

The policyholders' share equals 100 percent less the company's share, whereas the latter is equal to the company's share of net investment income divided by net investment income. The company's share of net investment income is the excess, if any, of net investment income over certain amounts, including "required interest," that are set aside to satisfy obligations to policyholders. Required interest with regard to an account is calculated by multiplying a specified account earnings rate by the mean of the reserves with regard to the account for the taxable year.

### Reasons for Change

The proration methodology currently used by some taxpayers may produce a company's share that greatly exceeds the company's economic interest in the net investment income earned by its separate account assets, generating controversy between life insurance companies and the IRS. The purposes of the proration regime would be better served if the company's share bore a more direct relationship to the company's actual economic interest in the account.

### Proposal

As under current law, required interest under the proposal would equal an earnings rate times the mean of reserves. For a separate account, the earnings rate would equal a gross earnings rate (net investment income of the account, divided by the mean of the account's assets), minus a company-retained percentage (amounts retained by the company from the account's net investment income, if any, divided by the mean of reserves). For this purpose, amounts retained by the company would be treated as funded proportionately by items included in net investment income and items not so included. It is intended that this formula would generally produce a company's share with regard to a separate account that approximates the ratio of the mean of the surplus attributable to the account to the mean of the account's assets.

The proposal would be effective for taxable years beginning after December 31, 2010.

# EXPAND PRO RATA INTEREST EXPENSE DISALLOWANCE FOR CORPORATE-OWNED LIFE INSURANCE (COLI)

## Current Law

In general, no Federal income tax is imposed on a policyholder with respect to the earnings credited under a life insurance or endowment contract, and Federal income tax generally is deferred with respect to earnings under an annuity contract (unless the annuity contract is owned by a person other than a natural person). In addition, amounts received under a life insurance contract by reason of the death of the insured generally are excluded from gross income of the recipient.

Interest on policy loans or other indebtedness with respect to life insurance, endowment or annuity contracts generally is not deductible, unless the insurance contract insures the life of a key person of the business. A key person includes a 20-percent owner of the business, as well as a limited number of the business' officers or employees. However, this interest disallowance rule applies to businesses only to the extent that the indebtedness can be traced to a life insurance, endowment or annuity contract.

In addition, the interest deductions of a business other than an insurance company are reduced to the extent the interest is allocable to unborrowed policy cash values based on a statutory formula. An exception to the pro rata interest disallowance applies with respect to contracts that cover individuals who are officers, directors, employees, or 20-percent owners of the taxpayer. In the case of both life and non-life insurance companies, special proration rules similarly require adjustments to prevent or limit the funding of tax-deductible reserve increases with tax preferred income, including earnings credited under life insurance, endowment and annuity contracts that would be subject to the pro rata interest disallowance rule if owned by a non-insurance company.

## Reasons for Change

Leveraged business can fund deductible interest expenses with tax-exempt or tax-deferred income credited under life insurance, endowment or annuity contracts insuring certain types of individuals. For example, these businesses frequently invest in investment-oriented insurance policies covering the lives of their employees, officers, directors or owners. These entities generally do not take out policy loans or other indebtedness that is secured or otherwise traceable to the insurance contracts. Instead, they borrow from depositors or other lenders, or issue bonds. Similar tax arbitrage benefits result when insurance companies invest in certain insurance contracts that cover the lives of their employees, officers, directors or 20-percent shareholders and fund deductible reserves with tax-exempt or tax-deferred income.

## Proposal

The proposal would repeal the exception from the pro rata interest expense disallowance rule for contracts covering employees, officers or directors, other than 20-percent owners of a business that is the owner or beneficiary of the contracts.

The proposal would apply to contracts entered into after the date of enactment.

**Tax Accounting Methods**

**DENY DEDUCTION FOR PUNITIVE DAMAGES**

<u>**Current Law**</u>

No deduction is allowed for a fine or similar penalty paid to a government for the violation of any law. If a taxpayer is convicted of a violation of the antitrust laws, or the taxpayer's plea of guilty or nolo contendere to such a violation is entered or accepted in a criminal proceeding, no deduction is allowed for two-thirds of any amount paid or incurred on a judgment or in settlement of a civil suit brought under section 4 of the Clayton Antitrust Act on account of such or any related antitrust violation. Where neither of these two provisions is applicable, a deduction is allowed for damages paid or incurred as ordinary and necessary expenses in carrying on any trade or business, regardless of whether such damages are compensatory or punitive.

<u>**Reasons for Change**</u>

The deductibility of punitive damage payments undermines the role of such damages in discouraging and penalizing certain undesirable actions or activities.

<u>**Proposal**</u>

No deduction would be allowed for punitive damages paid or incurred by the taxpayer, whether upon a judgment or in settlement of a claim. Where the liability for punitive damages is covered by insurance, such damages paid or incurred by the insurer would be included in the gross income of the insured person. The insurer would be required to report such payments to the insured person and to the Internal Revenue Service.

The proposal would apply to damages paid or incurred after December 31, 2010.

# REPEAL LOWER-OF-COST-OR-MARKET INVENTORY ACCOUNTING METHOD

## Current Law

Taxpayers required to maintain inventories are permitted to use a variety of methods to determine the cost of their ending inventories, including methods such as the last-in, first-out ("LIFO") method, the first-in, first-out ("FIFO") method, and the retail method. Taxpayers not using a LIFO method may write down the carrying values of their inventories by applying the lower-of-cost-or-market ("LCM") method and may write down the cost of "subnormal" goods (i.e., those that are unsalable at normal prices or unusable in the normal way because of damage, imperfection or other similar causes). Taxpayers using the retail method for tax currently are not required to use that method for financial statement reporting purposes.

## Reasons for Change

The allowance of inventory write-downs under the LCM and subnormal goods provisions is an exception from the realization principle, and is essentially a one-way mark-to-market regime that understates taxable income. Thus, a taxpayer is able to obtain a larger cost-of-goods-sold deduction by writing down an item of inventory if its replacement cost falls, but need not increase an item's inventory value if its replacement cost increases. This asymmetric treatment is unwarranted. Also, the market value used under LCM for tax purposes generally is the replacement or reproduction cost of an item of inventory, not the item's net realizable value, as is required under generally accepted financial accounting rules. While the operation of the retail method is technically symmetric, it also allows retailers to obtain deductions for write-downs below inventory cost because of normal and anticipated declines in retail prices.

## Proposal

The proposal would statutorily prohibit the use of the LCM and subnormal goods methods. Appropriate wash-sale rules also would be included to prevent taxpayers from circumventing the prohibition. The retail method would be allowed only if the taxpayer employs the method for purposes of financial accounting. The proposal would be treated as a change in the method of accounting for inventories, and any resulting section 481(a) adjustment generally would be included in income ratably over a four-year period beginning with the year of change.

The proposal would be effective for taxable years beginning after 12 months from the date of enactment.

**Modify Estate and Gift Tax Valuation Discounts and Make Other Reforms**

## REQUIRE CONSISTENCY IN VALUE FOR TRANSFER AND INCOME TAX PURPOSES

### Current Law

Section 1014 provides that the basis of property acquired from a decedent generally is the fair market value of the property on decedent's date of death. Similarly, property included in the decedent's gross estate for estate tax purposes generally must be valued at its fair market value on date of death. Although the same valuation standard applies to both provisions, current law does not explicitly require that the recipient's basis in that property be the same value at which that property was reported for estate tax purposes.

Section 1015 provides that the donee's basis in property received by gift during the life of the donor generally is the donor's adjusted basis in the property, increased by gift tax paid on the transfer. If, however, the donor's basis exceeds the fair market value of the property on the date of the gift, the donee's basis is limited to that fair market value for purposes of determining any subsequent loss.

Section 6034A imposes a consistency requirement – specifically, that the recipient of a distribution of income from a trust or estate must report on the recipient's own income tax return the exact information included on the Schedule K-1 of the trust's or estate's income tax return – but this provision applies only for income tax purposes, and the Schedule K-1 does not include basis information.

### Reasons for Change

Taxpayers should be required to take consistent positions in dealing with the Internal Revenue Service, whether or not principles of privity apply. If the logic underlying the new basis in property acquired on the death of the owner is that the new basis is the amount used to determine the decedent's estate tax liability, then the law should require that the same value be used by the recipient, unless that value is in excess of the accurate value. In the case of property transferred on death or by gift during life, often the executor of the estate or the donor, respectively, will be in the best position to ensure that the recipient receives the necessary information that will determine that recipient's basis in the transferred property.

### Proposal

This proposal would require both consistency and a reporting requirement. The basis of property received by reason of death under section 1014 would have to equal the value of that property for estate tax purposes. The basis of property received by gift during the life of the donor would have to equal the donor's basis determined under section 1015. This proposal would require that the basis of the property in the hands of the recipient be no greater than the value of that property as determined for estate or gift tax purposes (subject to subsequent adjustments). A reporting requirement would be imposed on the executor of the decedent's estate and on the donor of a lifetime gift to provide the necessary information to both the recipient and the IRS. A grant of regulatory authority would be included to provide details about the implementation and administration of these requirements, including rules for situations in which no estate tax return is required to be filed or gifts are excluded from gift tax under section 2503, for situations in which the surviving joint tenant or other recipient may have better information than the executor, and for the timing of the required reporting in the event of adjustments to the reported value subsequent to the filing of an estate or gift tax return.

The proposal would be effective as of the date of enactment.

## MODIFY RULES ON VALUATION DISCOUNTS

### Current Law

The fair market value of property transferred, whether on the death or during the life of the transferor, generally is subject to estate or gift tax at the time of the transfer. Sections 2701 through 2704 of the Internal Revenue Code were enacted to prevent the reduction of taxes through the use of "estate freezes" and other techniques designed to reduce the value of the transferor's taxable estate and discount the value of the taxable transfer to the beneficiaries of the transferor when the economic benefit to the beneficiaries is not reduced by these techniques. Generally, section 2704(b) provides that certain "applicable restrictions" (that would normally justify discounts in the value of the interests transferred) are to be ignored in valuing interests in family-controlled entities if those interests are transferred (either by gift or on death) to or for the benefit of other family members. The application of these special rules results in an increase in the transfer tax value of those interests above the price that a hypothetical willing buyer would pay a willing seller, because section 2704(b) generally directs an appraiser to ignore the rights and restrictions that would otherwise support significant discounts for lack of marketability and control.

### Reasons for Change

Judicial decisions and the enactment of new statutes in most states have, in effect, made section 2704(b) inapplicable in many situations, specifically, by recharacterizing restrictions such that they no longer fall within the definition of an "applicable restriction". In addition, the Internal Revenue Service has identified additional arrangements designed to circumvent the application of section 2704.

### Proposal

This proposal would create an additional category of restrictions ("disregarded restrictions") that would be ignored in valuing an interest in a family-controlled entity transferred to a member of the family if, after the transfer, the restriction will lapse or may be removed by the transferor and/or the transfer's family. Specifically, the transferred interest would be valued by substituting for the disregarded restrictions certain assumptions to be specified in regulations. Disregarded restrictions would include limitations on a holder's right to liquidate that holder's interest that are more restrictive than a standard identified in regulations. A disregarded restriction also would include any limitation on a transferee's ability to be admitted as a full partner or holder of an equity interest in the entity. For purposes of determining whether a restriction may be removed by member(s) of the family after the transfer, certain interests (to be identified in regulations) held by charities or others who are not family members of the transferor would be deemed to be held by the family. Regulatory authority would be granted, including the ability to create safe harbors to permit taxpayers to draft the governing documents of a family-controlled entity so as to avoid the application of section 2704 if certain standards are met. This proposal would make conforming clarifications with regard to the interaction of this proposal with the transfer tax marital and charitable deductions.

This proposal would apply to transfers after the date of enactment of property subject to restrictions created after October 8, 1990 (the effective date of section 2704).

## REQUIRE MINIMUM TERM FOR GRANTOR RETAINED ANNUITY TRUSTS (GRATS)

### Current Law

Section 2702 provides that, if an interest in a trust is transferred to a family member, the value of any interest retained by the grantor is valued at zero for purposes of determining the transfer tax value of the gift to the family member(s). This rule does not apply if the retained interest is a "qualified interest". A fixed annuity, such as the annuity interest retained by the grantor of a GRAT, is one form of qualified interest, so the gift of the remainder interest in the GRAT is determined by deducting the present value of the retained annuity during the GRAT term from the fair market value of the property contributed to the trust.

Generally, a GRAT is an irrevocable trust funded with assets expected to appreciate in value, in which the grantor retains an annuity interest for a term of years that the grantor expects to survive. At the end of that term, the assets then remaining in the trust are transferred to (or held in further trust for) the beneficiaries, who generally are descendants of the grantor. If the grantor dies during the GRAT term, however, the trust assets (at least the portion needed to produce the retained annuity) are included in the grantor's gross estate for estate tax purposes. In this event, although the beneficiaries will own the remaining trust assets, the estate tax benefit of creating the GRAT (specifically, the tax-free transfer of the appreciation during the GRAT term in excess of the annuity payments) is not realized.

### Reasons for Change

GRATs have proven to be a popular and efficient technique for transferring wealth while minimizing the gift tax cost of transfers, providing that the grantor survives the GRAT term and the trust assets do not depreciate in value. The greater the appreciation, the greater the transfer tax benefit achieved. Taxpayers have become more adept at maximizing the benefit of this technique, often by minimizing the term of the GRAT (thus reducing the risk of the grantor's death during the term), in many cases to 2 years, and by retaining annuity interests significant enough to reduce the gift tax value of the remainder interest to zero or to a number small enough to generate only a minimal gift tax liability.

### Proposal

This proposal would require, in effect, some downside risk in the use of this technique by imposing the requirement that a GRAT have a minimum term of 10 years.[5] Although a minimum term would not prevent "zeroing-out" the gift tax value of the remainder interest, it would increase the risk of the grantor's death during the GRAT term and the resulting loss of any anticipated transfer tax benefit.

This proposal would apply to trusts created after the date of enactment.

---

[5] Cf. section 673 as applicable to a so-called *Clifford* trust created before or on March 1, 1986, with a 10-year minimum term.

## MODIFY ALTERNATIVE FUEL MIXTURE CREDIT

### Current Law

The Code provides excise tax credits for alternative fuel and alternative fuel mixtures. Alternative fuel means liquefied petroleum gas, P Series fuels (as defined by the Secretary of Energy under 42 U.S.C. sec. 13211(2)), compressed or liquefied natural gas, liquefied hydrogen, certain liquid fuel derived from coal through the Fischer-Tropsch process, compressed or liquefied gas derived from biomass, and liquid fuel derived from biomass, but does not include ethanol, methanol, or biodiesel. The alternative fuel credit is 50 cents per gallon for liquid fuel and 50 cents per gasoline gallon equivalent for nonliquid fuel. The alternative fuel credit is available only for fuel sold by the taxpayer for use as a fuel in a motor vehicle or motorboat or so used by the taxpayer. The alternative fuel mixture credit is computed at the same rate on each gallon of alternative fuel used in producing a mixture of alternative fuel and taxable fuel for sale or use in the taxpayer's trade or business. The mixture must be sold by its producer for use as a fuel or used as a fuel by the producer. Both credits are allowed against fuel excise tax liability. In addition, a person may file a claim for payment equal to the amount of the alternative fuel and alternative fuel mixture credits. Except in the case of liquefied hydrogen, the credits expire on December 31, 2009.

### Reasons for Change

Alternative fuels include liquid byproducts derived from the processing of paper or pulp (known as "black liquor" when derived from the kraft process), which paper companies burn to produce energy in their mills. Certain paper companies, to take advantage of the alternative fuels mixture credit, have recently begun mixing diesel fuel with black liquor, burning the mixture, and claiming the alternative fuel mixture credit. This is resulting in substantial revenue losses and provides a windfall to the paper industry.

### Proposal

The Administration proposes to limit the credit for mixtures containing alternative fuel derived from the processing of paper or pulp to mixtures that are sold for use or used as fuel in a motor vehicle or motorboat. Accordingly, black liquor mixtures used as a fuel in paper processing would no longer be eligible for the credit.

The change would be effective after the date of enactment.

# APPENDIX: EXTENDING CURRENT POLICIES

The first step in addressing the nation's fiscal problems is to be upfront about them – and to establish an honest baseline that measures where we are before new policies are enacted. The Administration's Budget does so by adjusting the Budget Enforcement Act (BEA) baseline to reflect the true cost of the current policy path. The BEA baseline, which is commonly used in budgeting and is defined in a now expired statute, with some exceptions reflects the projected receipts level under current law. But, under current law, relief from the AMT would expire at the end of this year, causing millions of Americans to begin paying this additional tax, and, furthermore, the 2001 and 2003 tax cuts would expire entirely at the end of 2010. These expirations were not written into law for policy reasons; instead, they reflect decisions made to artificially reduce the cost estimates of AMT relief and the 2001 and 2003 tax cuts to fit these policies within certain budget process rules. Because of this, the BEA's "current law" baseline is not an accurate reflection of what it would mean to continue forward with current policies. The Administration's Budget uses an adjusted tax baseline that continues AMT relief and the 2001 and 2003 tax cuts, so as to project future receipts under current policy and to better measure the effects of the Administration's proposed policy changes.

***Index to inflation the 2009 parameters of the AMT as enacted in the American Recovery and Reinvestment Act of 2009.*** The Administration's baseline projection of current policy reflects annual indexation of the AMT exemption amounts in effect for taxable year 2009 ($46,700 for single taxpayers, $70,950 for married taxpayers filing a joint return and surviving spouses, and $35,475 for married taxpayers filing a separate return and for estates and trusts); the income thresholds for the 28-percent rate ($87,500 for married taxpayers filing a separate return and $175,000 for all other taxpayers); and the income thresholds for the phaseout of the exemption amounts ($150,000 for married taxpayers filing a joint return and surviving spouses, $112,500 for single taxpayers, and $75,000 for married taxpayers filing a separate return). The baseline projection of current policy also extends AMT relief for nonrefundable personal credits.

***Continue the 2001 and 2003 tax cuts.*** Most of the tax reductions enacted in 2001 and 2003 expire on December 31, 2010. The Administration's baseline projection of current policy continues all of these expiring provisions except for repeal of estate and generation-skipping transfer taxes. Estate and gift taxes are assumed to be extended at parameters in effect for calendar year 2009 (a top rate of 45 percent and an exemption amount of $3.5 million).

# TABLES OF REVENUE ESTIMATES

Revenue estimates begin on next page.

Table 1  Revenue Estimates of FY 2010 Budget Proposals 1/ 2/

Fiscal Years
(in millions of dollars)

| | 2009 | 2010 | 2011 | 2012 | 2013 | 2014 | 2015 | 2016 | 2017 | 2018 | 2019 | 2010-2014 | 2010-2019 |
|---|---|---|---|---|---|---|---|---|---|---|---|---|---|
| **Tax Cuts for Families and Individuals** | | | | | | | | | | | | | |
| Provide the making work pay tax credit 3/ | 0 | 0 | -31,080 | -61,668 | -61,949 | -62,233 | -62,658 | -63,256 | -63,626 | -64,052 | -64,488 | -216,930 | -535,010 |
| Expand the earned income tax credit 3/ | 0 | 0 | -17 | -2,666 | -2,601 | -2,575 | -2,610 | -2,659 | -2,708 | -2,762 | -2,821 | -7,859 | -21,419 |
| Expand the refundability of the child tax credit 3/ | 0 | 0 | 0 | -8,822 | -8,707 | -8,674 | -8,766 | -8,859 | -8,944 | -9,039 | -9,142 | -26,203 | -70,953 |
| Expand the saver's credit and provide for automatic enrollment in  RAs  3/ | 0 | 0 | -232 | -3,153 | -5,054 | -6,366 | -7,451 | -8,363 | -9,083 | -9,689 | -10,226 | -14,805 | -59,617 |
| Provide the American opportunity tax credit 3/ | 0 | 0 | -594 | -4,350 | -4,931 | -5,526 | -5,879 | -6,316 | -6,689 | -6,985 | -7,246 | -15,401 | -48,516 |
| **Subtotal, tax cuts for families and individuals** | **0** | **0** | **-31,923** | **-80,659** | **-83,242** | **-85,374** | **-87,364** | **-89,453** | **-91,050** | **-92,527** | **-93,923** | **-281,198** | **-735,515** |
| **Tax Cuts for Businesses** | | | | | | | | | | | | | |
| Eliminate capital gains taxation on investments in small business stock | 0 | 0 | 0 | 0 | 0 | -134 | -344 | -700 | -1,187 | -1,562 | -1,908 | -134 | -5,835 |
| Make the research & experimentation tax credit permanent | 0 | -3,111 | -5,486 | -6,142 | -6,785 | -7,384 | -7,960 | -8,530 | -9,103 | -9,680 | -10,281 | -28,908 | -74,462 |
| Expand net operating loss carryback | -27,800 | -35,700 | 10,700 | 10,200 | 7,900 | 5,600 | 3,900 | 2,700 | 1,800 | 1,300 | 900 | -1,300 | 9,300 |
| **Subtotal, tax cuts for businesses** | **-27,800** | **-38,811** | **5,214** | **4,058** | **1,115** | **-1,918** | **-4,404** | **-6,530** | **-8,490** | **-9,942** | **-11,289** | **-30,342** | **-70,997** |
| **Modify Federal Aviation Administration Financing** | **0** | **0** | **-7,225** | **-7,599** | **-7,980** | **-8,260** | **-8,559** | **-8,869** | **-9,190** | **-9,527** | **-9,873** | **-31,064** | **-77,082** |
| **Continue Certain Expiring Provisions Through Calendar Year 2010  3/** | **-28** | **-6,402** | **-5,449** | **-668** | **-593** | **-617** | **-782** | **-860** | **-588** | **-595** | **-689** | **-13,729** | **-17,243** |
| **Other Revenue Changes and Loophole Closers** | | | | | | | | | | | | | |
| Reinstate Superfund excise taxes | 0 | 0 | 754 | 1,024 | 1,130 | 1,196 | 1,247 | 1,297 | 1,352 | 1,419 | 1,490 | 4,104 | 10,909 |
| Reinstate Superfund environmental income tax | 0 | 0 | 443 | 608 | 625 | 638 | 658 | 682 | 704 | 730 | 760 | 2,314 | 5,848 |
| Tax carried (profit) interests as ordinary income | 0 | 0 | 2,585 | 3,811 | 3,860 | 3,463 | 2,899 | 2,345 | 1,869 | 1,479 | 1,167 | 13,719 | 23,478 |
| Codify economic substance doctrine | 5 | 58 | 112 | 202 | 308 | 426 | 546 | 642 | 724 | 809 | 901 | 1,106 | 4,728 |
| Repeal LIFO method of accounting for inventories | 0 | 0 | 0 | 2,992 | 6,748 | 8,082 | 8,431 | 8,590 | 8,545 | 8,630 | 9,036 | 17,822 | 61,054 |
| *Reform U.S. international tax system:* | | | | | | | | | | | | | |
| Reform business entity classification rules for foreign entities | 0 | 0 | 4,932 | 8,556 | 9,147 | 9,597 | 9,917 | 10,267 | 10,741 | 11,352 | 12,000 | 32,232 | 86,509 |
| Defer deduction of expenses, except R&E expenses, related to deferred income | 0 | 0 | 3,754 | 6,321 | 6,434 | 6,545 | 6,731 | 6,992 | 7,311 | 7,732 | 8,230 | 23,054 | 60,050 |
| Reform foreign tax credit: Determine the foreign tax credit on a pooling basis | 0 | 0 | 1,531 | 2,578 | 2,624 | 2,669 | 2,745 | 2,852 | 2,982 | 3,154 | 3,357 | 9,402 | 24,492 |
| Reform foreign tax credit: Prevent splitting of foreign income and foreign taxes | 0 | 0 | 999 | 1,792 | 1,968 | 2,095 | 2,194 | 2,277 | 2,348 | 2,408 | 2,461 | 6,854 | 18,542 |
| Limit shifting of income through intangible property transfers | 0 | 0 | 37 | 102 | 169 | 240 | 314 | 391 | 471 | 556 | 644 | 548 | 2,924 |
| Limit earnings stripping by expatriated entities | 0 | 0 | 70 | 120 | 126 | 132 | 139 | 146 | 153 | 161 | 169 | 448 | 1,216 |
| Prevent repatriation of earnings in certain cross-border reorganizations | 0 | 0 | 19 | 31 | 32 | 33 | 34 | 35 | 36 | 38 | 39 | 115 | 297 |
| Repeal 80/20 company rules | 0 | 0 | 86 | 121 | 129 | 135 | 139 | 144 | 151 | 160 | 169 | 471 | 1,234 |
| Prevent the avoidance of dividend withholding taxes | 0 | 0 | 373 | 281 | 126 | 99 | 100 | 101 | 104 | 109 | 114 | 879 | 1,407 |
| Modify tax rules for dual capacity taxpayers | 0 | 0 | 260 | 449 | 471 | 492 | 515 | 538 | 562 | 588 | 615 | 1,672 | 4,490 |
| Combat under-reporting of income through use of accounts and entities in offshore jurisdictions | 0 | 0 | 1,617 | -53 | -115 | 449 | 769 | 843 | 876 | 914 | 953 | 4,380 | 8,735 |
| *subtotal, reform U.S. international tax system* | *0* | *0* | *13,678* | *20,298* | *21,111* | *22,486* | *23,597* | *24,586* | *25,735* | *27,172* | *28,751* | *80,055* | *209,896* |
| Require information reporting for rental property expense payments | 0 | 175 | 265 | 280 | 290 | 305 | 315 | 330 | 340 | 360 | 375 | 1,315 | 3,035 |
| *Eliminate oil and gas company preferences:* | | | | | | | | | | | | | |
| Levy tax on certain offshore oil and gas production | 0 | 0 | 500 | 500 | 500 | 600 | 600 | 600 | 600 | 700 | 700 | 2,100 | 5,300 |
| Repeal credit for enhanced oil recovery projects 4/ | 0 | 0 | 0 | 0 | 0 | 0 | 0 | 0 | 0 | 0 | 0 | 0 | 0 |
| Repeal credit for production from marginal wells 4/ | 0 | 0 | 0 | 0 | 0 | 0 | 0 | 0 | 0 | 0 | 0 | 0 | 0 |
| Repeal expensing of intangible drilling costs | 0 | 0 | 347 | 595 | 526 | 395 | 269 | 226 | 237 | 266 | 488 | 1,863 | 3,349 |
| Repeal deduction for tertiary injectants | 0 | 0 | 5 | 9 | 9 | 8 | 7 | 6 | 6 | 6 | 6 | 31 | 62 |
| Repeal passive loss exemption for working interests in oil and gas properties | 0 | 0 | 2 | 5 | 6 | 6 | 6 | 6 | 6 | 6 | 6 | 19 | 49 |
| Repeal percentage depletion | 0 | 0 | 316 | 752 | 925 | 960 | 996 | 1,033 | 1,065 | 1,091 | 1,113 | 2,953 | 8,251 |
| Repeal domestic manufacturing deduction for oil and gas production | 0 | 0 | 757 | 1,310 | 1,392 | 1,464 | 1,531 | 1,600 | 1,670 | 1,745 | 1,823 | 4,923 | 13,292 |
| Increase the amortization period for geological and geophysical costs to seven years | 0 | 0 | 41 | 154 | 240 | 233 | 187 | 140 | 91 | 56 | 47 | 668 | 1,189 |
| *subtotal, eliminate oil and gas company preferences* | *0* | *0* | *1,968* | *3,325* | *3,598* | *3,666* | *3,596* | *3,611* | *3,675* | *3,870* | *4,183* | *12,557* | *31,492* |
| Eliminate the advanced earned income tax credit 3/ | 0 | 125 | 76 | 77 | 78 | 81 | 83 | 85 | 87 | 89 | 91 | 437 | 872 |
| **Subtotal, other revenue changes and loophole closers** | **5** | **2,840** | **19,881** | **32,617** | **37,748** | **40,343** | **41,372** | **42,168** | **43,031** | **44,558** | **46,754** | **133,429** | **351,312** |

| | | | | | | | Fiscal Years | | | | | | |
|---|---|---|---|---|---|---|---|---|---|---|---|---|---|
| | | | | | | | (in millions of dollars) | | | | | | |
| | 2009 | 2010 | 2011 | 2012 | 2013 | 2014 | 2015 | 2016 | 2017 | 2018 | 2019 | 2010-2014 | 2010-2019 |
| **Upper-Income Tax Provisions Dedicated to Deficit Reduction** | | | | | | | | | | | | | |
| Reinstate the 39.6% rate | 0 | 0 | 12,939 | 25,003 | 27,869 | 30,537 | 32,941 | 36,007 | 38,571 | 41,010 | 44,268 | 96,348 | 289,145 |
| Reinstate the 36% rate for taxpayers with income over $250,000 (married) and $200,000 (single) | 0 | 0 | 1,645 | 2,622 | 2,929 | 3,232 | 3,548 | 3,305 | 3,795 | 4,492 | 4,847 | 10,428 | 30,415 |
| Reinstate the limitation on itemized deductions for taxpayers with income over $250,000 (married) and $200,000 (single) | 0 | 0 | 5,334 | 11,659 | 13,308 | 14,568 | 15,736 | 16,914 | 18,094 | 19,245 | 20,417 | 44,869 | 135,275 |
| Reinstate the personal exemption phaseout (PEP) for taxpayers with income over $250,000 (married) and $200,000 (single) | 0 | 0 | 1,624 | 3,582 | 4,120 | 4,533 | 4,946 | 5,350 | 5,756 | 6,187 | 6,654 | 13,859 | 42,752 |
| Impose a 20% rate on dividends and capital gains for taxpayers with income over $250,000 (married) and $200,000 (single) | -182 | 600 | 6,641 | 3,672 | 7,412 | 12,060 | 14,832 | 15,970 | 17,495 | 18,873 | 20,235 | 30,385 | 117,790 |
| Subtotal, upper-income tax provisions dedicated to deficit reduction | -182 | 600 | 28,183 | 46,538 | 55,638 | 64,930 | 72,003 | 77,546 | 83,711 | 89,807 | 96,421 | 195,889 | 615,377 |
| **User Fees** | | | | | | | | | | | | | |
| Preserve cost-sharing of inland waterways capital costs | 0 | 75 | 100 | 68 | 79 | 89 | 156 | 155 | 183 | 182 | 180 | 411 | 1,267 |
| **Trade Proposals** | | | | | | | | | | | | | |
| Promote trade | 0 | 0 | -2 | -5 | -9 | -13 | -18 | -25 | -30 | -35 | -37 | -29 | -174 |
| **Other Initiatives** | | | | | | | | | | | | | |
| Implement unemployment insurance integrity legislation | 0 | 0 | 34 | 29 | -20 | -4 | -166 | -168 | -174 | -1,023 | -413 | 39 | -1,905 |
| Restructure assistance to New York City: | | | | | | | | | | | | | |
| Provide tax incentives for transportation infrastructure | 0 | -200 | -200 | -200 | -200 | -200 | -200 | -200 | -200 | -200 | -200 | -1,000 | -2,000 |
| Revise terrorism risk insurance program | 0 | 0 | -39 | -493 | -150 | -317 | -511 | -576 | -522 | -416 | -285 | -999 | -3,309 |
| Levy payments to Federal contractors with delinquent tax debt: | | | | | | | | | | | | | |
| Improve debt collection administrative procedures | 0 | 77 | 115 | 119 | 124 | 109 | 113 | 118 | 122 | 127 | 132 | 544 | 1,156 |
| Increase levy authority to 100% for vendor payments | 0 | 61 | 87 | 86 | 90 | 78 | 92 | 85 | 88 | 92 | 96 | 402 | 845 |
| subtotal, levy payments to Federal contractors with delinquent tax debt | 0 | 138 | 202 | 205 | 214 | 187 | 195 | 203 | 210 | 219 | 228 | 946 | 2,001 |
| Subtotal, other initiatives | 0 | -62 | -3 | -459 | -156 | -334 | -682 | -741 | -686 | -1,420 | -670 | -1,014 | -5,213 |
| Total Effect of FY 2010 Budget Tax Proposals Relative to Current Policy | -28,005 | -41,760 | 8,776 | -6,109 | 2,600 | 8,846 | 11,722 | 13,391 | 16,891 | 20,501 | 26,874 | -27,647 | 61,732 |

Department of the Treasury

Notes:

1 / Presentation in this table does not reflect the order in which these proposals were estimated.

2 / Appendix B details the budgetary impact of extending tax policies currently in effect relative to current law. These extensions are estimated before the other policy proposals that follow in this table.

3 / This provision affects both receipts and outlays. The combined effects are shown here. The outlay effects included in these estimates are detailed in Appendix C.

4 / This provision is estimated to have zero receipt effect under the Administration's current projections for energy prices.

Appendix A  Revenue Estimates of Proposals Dedicated to the Health Reform Reserve Fund 1/

| | 2009 | 2010 | 2011 | 2012 | 2013 | 2014 | 2015 | 2016 | 2017 | 2018 | 2019 | 2010-2014 | 2010-2019 |
|---|---|---|---|---|---|---|---|---|---|---|---|---|---|
| | | | | | | (in millions of dollars) | | | | | | | |
| Limit the tax rate at which itemized deductions reduce tax liability to 28% | 0 | 0 | 9,241 | 24,945 | 27,687 | 29,647 | 31,386 | 33,091 | 34,911 | 36,873 | 38,878 | 91,520 | 266,659 |
| **Reduce the tax gap and make reforms:** | | | | | | | | | | | | | |
| *Expand information reporting:* | | | | | | | | | | | | | |
| Require information reporting for private separate accounts of life insurance companies | | 0 | 2 | 5 | 4 | 3 | 2 | 1 | 1 | 1 | 1 | 14 | 20 |
| Require information reporting on payments to corporations | | 84 | 612 | 777 | 924 | 983 | 1,040 | 1,095 | 1,152 | 1,212 | 1,275 | 3,380 | 9,154 |
| Require a certified Taxpayer Identification Number from contractors | | 17 | 44 | 63 | 72 | 76 | 79 | 83 | 86 | 90 | 94 | 272 | 704 |
| Require increased information reporting for certain government payments | | 18 | 66 | 68 | 19 | 10 | 10 | 0 | 0 | 0 | 0 | 181 | 191 |
| Increase information return penalties | | 20 | 34 | 35 | 35 | 36 | 42 | 43 | 43 | 44 | 44 | 160 | 376 |
| subtotal, expand information reporting | | 139 | 758 | 948 | 1,054 | 1,108 | 1,173 | 1,222 | 1,282 | 1,347 | 1,414 | 4,007 | 10,445 |
| *Improve compliance by businesses:* | | | | | | | | | | | | | |
| Require E-filing by certain large organizations | | | | | | No Revenue Effect | | | | | | | |
| Implement standards clarifying when employee leasing companies can be held liable for their clients' Federal employment taxes | 0 | 3 | 5 | 5 | 5 | 6 | 6 | 6 | 7 | 7 | 7 | 24 | 57 |
| subtotal, improve compliance by businesses | 0 | 3 | 5 | 5 | 5 | 6 | 6 | 6 | 7 | 7 | 7 | 24 | 57 |
| *Strengthen tax administration:* | | | | | | | | | | | | | |
| Allow assessment of criminal restitution as tax | | 0 | 2 | 3 | 4 | 4 | 4 | 4 | 4 | 4 | 4 | 13 | 33 |
| Revise offer-in-compromise application rules | | 3 | 3 | 3 | 3 | 4 | 3 | 3 | 3 | 3 | 3 | 15 | 30 |
| Expand IRS access to information in the National Directory of New Hires for tax administration purposes | | | | | | No Revenue Effect | | | | | | | |
| Make repeated willful failure to file a tax return a felony | | 0 | 0 | 0 | 0 | 1 | 1 | 1 | 2 | 2 | 2 | 2 | 10 |
| Facilitate tax compliance with local jurisdictions | | 0 | 0 | 0 | 0 | 0 | 1 | 1 | 1 | 1 | 1 | 0 | 5 |
| Extension of statute of limitations where state adjustment affects federal tax liability | | 5 | 8 | 8 | 8 | 8 | 9 | 10 | 10 | 10 | 10 | 37 | 86 |
| Improve investigative disclosure statute | | 0 | 0 | 1 | 1 | 1 | 1 | 1 | 2 | 2 | 2 | 3 | 11 |
| Expand required electronic filing by tax preparers | | | | | | No Revenue Effect | | | | | | | |
| subtotal, strengthen tax administration | 0 | 8 | 13 | 15 | 17 | 17 | 19 | 20 | 22 | 22 | 22 | 70 | 175 |
| *Expand penalties:* | | | | | | | | | | | | | |
| Clarify that bad check penalty applies to electronic checks and other payment forms | | 1 | 2 | 2 | 2 | 3 | 3 | 3 | 3 | 4 | 4 | 10 | 27 |
| Impose a penalty on failure to comply with electronic filing requirements | 0 | 0 | 0 | 0 | 0 | 1 | 1 | 1 | 2 | 2 | 2 | 1 | 9 |
| subtotal, expand penalties | 0 | 1 | 2 | 2 | 2 | 4 | 4 | 4 | 5 | 6 | 6 | 11 | 36 |
| **Subtotal, reduce the tax gap and make reforms** | 0 | 151 | 778 | 970 | 1,078 | 1,135 | 1,202 | 1,252 | 1,316 | 1,382 | 1,449 | 4,112 | 10,713 |
| **Make reforms to close tax loopholes:** | | | | | | | | | | | | | |
| *Financial institutions and products:* | | | | | | | | | | | | | |
| Require accrual of income on forward sale of corporate stock | 0 | 0 | 2 | 7 | 13 | 20 | 28 | 33 | 36 | 38 | 40 | 42 | 217 |
| Require ordinary treatment for certain dealers of equity options and commodities | 47 | 192 | 267 | 214 | 226 | 240 | 254 | 270 | 286 | 303 | 321 | 1,139 | 2,573 |
| Modify the definition of control for purposes of section 249 deduction limit | 12 | 62 | 114 | 120 | 128 | 135 | 143 | 152 | 161 | 171 | 181 | 559 | 1,367 |
| subtotal, financial products | 59 | 254 | 383 | 341 | 367 | 395 | 425 | 455 | 483 | 512 | 542 | 1,740 | 4,157 |
| *Insurance companies and products:* | | | | | | | | | | | | | |
| Modify rules that apply to sales of life insurance contracts | | 0 | 24 | 74 | 80 | 88 | 94 | 101 | 108 | 116 | 127 | 266 | 812 |
| Modify dividends-received deduction for life insurance company separate accounts | | 0 | 115 | 296 | 331 | 385 | 419 | 439 | 463 | 485 | 511 | 1,127 | 3,444 |
| Expand pro rata interest expense disallowance for corporate-owned life insurance | 0 | 318 | 619 | 786 | 891 | 897 | 909 | 952 | 995 | 1,037 | 1,069 | 3,511 | 8,473 |
| subtotal, insurance companies and products | 0 | 318 | 758 | 1,156 | 1,302 | 1,370 | 1,422 | 1,492 | 1,566 | 1,638 | 1,707 | 4,904 | 12,729 |
| *Tax accounting methods:* | | | | | | | | | | | | | |
| Deny deduction for punitive damages | | 0 | 27 | 34 | 32 | 33 | 34 | 35 | 36 | 38 | 38 | 126 | 307 |
| Repeal lower-of-cost-or-market inventory accounting method | 0 | 0 | 0 | 950 | 1,882 | 1,163 | 1,173 | 233 | 243 | 254 | 266 | 3,995 | 6,164 |
| subtotal, tax accounting methods | 0 | 0 | 27 | 984 | 1,914 | 1,196 | 1,207 | 268 | 279 | 292 | 304 | 4,121 | 6,471 |
| *Modify estate and gift tax valuation discounts and make other reforms:* | | | | | | | | | | | | | |
| Require consistency in value for transfer and income tax purposes | | 40 | 135 | 171 | 182 | 192 | 204 | 216 | 229 | 243 | 258 | 720 | 1,870 |
| Modify rules on valuation discounts | | 667 | 1,419 | 1,543 | 1,692 | 1,848 | 2,012 | 2,184 | 2,364 | 2,555 | 2,754 | 7,169 | 19,038 |
| Require a minimum term for grantor retained annuity trusts (GRATs) | | 29 | 61 | 123 | 191 | 263 | 340 | 422 | 510 | 605 | 706 | 667 | 3,250 |
| subtotal, modify estate and gift tax valuation discounts and make other reforms | 0 | 736 | 1,615 | 1,837 | 2,065 | 2,303 | 2,556 | 2,822 | 3,103 | 3,403 | 3,718 | 8,556 | 24,158 |
| **Subtotal, make reforms to close tax loopholes** | 59 | 1,308 | 2,783 | 4,318 | 5,648 | 5,264 | 5,610 | 5,037 | 5,431 | 5,845 | 6,271 | 19,321 | 47,515 |
| Modify alternative fuel mixture credit | 533 | 702 | 0 | 0 | 0 | 0 | 0 | 0 | 0 | 0 | 0 | 702 | 702 |
| **Total Effect Proposals Dedicated to the Health Reform Reserve Fund** | 592 | 2,161 | 12,802 | 30,233 | 34,413 | 36,046 | 38,198 | 39,380 | 41,658 | 44,100 | 46,598 | 115,655 | 325,589 |

Department of the Treasury

Note:

1 / Appendix B details the budgetary impact of extending tax policies currently in effect relative to current law. These extensions are estimated before the other policy proposals that follow in this table and Table 1.

## Appendix B: Bridge from Budget Enforcement Act Baseline to Current Policy Baseline 1/

| | 2009 | 2010 | 2011 | 2012 | 2013 | 2014 | 2015 | 2016 | 2017 | 2018 | 2019 | 2010-2014 | 2010-2019 |
|---|---|---|---|---|---|---|---|---|---|---|---|---|---|
| | | | | | | (in millions of dollars) | | | | | | | |
| *Adjustments to provisions to reflect current policy baseline:* | | | | | | | | | | | | | |
| Alternative minimum tax | 0 | -14,056 | -69,054 | -33,944 | -39,361 | -46,408 | -54,626 | -63,500 | -73,289 | -84,685 | -97,166 | -202,823 | -576,089 |
| Estate tax | -483 | 3,071 | 1,095 | -13,549 | -16,940 | -19,947 | -21,709 | -23,420 | -24,891 | -26,485 | -28,293 | -46,270 | -171,068 |
| Tax rates on dividends | 316 | -5,458 | -27,801 | -6,568 | -18,264 | -30,886 | -38,127 | -39,573 | -41,116 | -42,716 | -44,449 | -88,977 | -294,958 |
| Tax rates on capital gains | 0 | -1,958 | -8,863 | -3,016 | -5,777 | -9,063 | -11,054 | -12,106 | -13,349 | -14,164 | -14,743 | -28,677 | -94,093 |
| Expensing for small business | 0 | 0 | -2,505 | -5,428 | -4,277 | -3,529 | -2,998 | -2,599 | -2,154 | -1,832 | -1,745 | -15,739 | -27,067 |
| Marginal individual income tax rates | 0 | 0 | -84,563 | -129,915 | -140,605 | -148,877 | -157,523 | -166,428 | -175,576 | -185,177 | -195,209 | -503,960 | -1,383,873 |
| Pease cutback of itemized deductions | 0 | 0 | -4,730 | -10,034 | -11,173 | -12,205 | -13,181 | -14,177 | -15,174 | -16,185 | -17,185 | -38,142 | -114,044 |
| Personal exemption phase out | 0 | 0 | -1,568 | -3,324 | -3,700 | -4,055 | -4,431 | -4,794 | -5,166 | -5,600 | -6,034 | -12,647 | -38,672 |
| Child tax credit 2/ | 0 | 0 | -3,305 | -27,619 | -27,761 | -27,859 | -28,004 | -28,250 | -28,359 | -28,531 | -28,682 | -86,544 | -228,370 |
| 15% income tax bracket for married taxpayers | 0 | 0 | -13,718 | -20,408 | -21,733 | -22,836 | -23,702 | -24,742 | -25,742 | -26,669 | -27,626 | -78,695 | -207,176 |
| Standard deduction for married taxpayers | 0 | 0 | -2,823 | -5,812 | -6,232 | -6,558 | -6,877 | -7,128 | -7,391 | -7,826 | -8,278 | -21,425 | -58,925 |
| EITC marriage penalty relief and simplification 2/ | 0 | 0 | 659 | -1,958 | -1,851 | -1,781 | -1,769 | -1,772 | -1,772 | -1,774 | -1,777 | -4,931 | -13,795 |
| Tax incentives for higher education | 0 | 3 | -736 | -1,347 | -1,419 | -1,489 | -1,561 | -1,636 | -1,716 | -1,800 | -1,886 | -4,988 | -13,587 |
| Employer-provided child care credit | 0 | 6 | -13 | -18 | -19 | -20 | -21 | -22 | -23 | -24 | -25 | -64 | -179 |
| Child dependent care credit | 0 | 0 | -247 | -624 | -637 | -651 | -664 | -677 | -689 | -702 | -714 | -2,159 | -5,605 |
| Federal income tax benefits for adoption | 0 | 0 | -238 | -382 | -398 | -414 | -429 | -447 | -464 | -483 | -502 | -1,432 | -3,757 |
| **Total Adjustments to BEA Baseline** | **-167** | **-18,392** | **-218,410** | **-263,946** | **-300,147** | **-336,578** | **-366,676** | **-391,271** | **-416,871** | **-444,653** | **-474,314** | **-1,137,473** | **-3,231,258** |

Department of the Treasury

Notes:

1 / Proposals in this table are estimated before the proposals in Table 1 and Appendix A.

2 / This provision affects both receipts and outlays. The combined effects included in these estimates are shown here. The outlay effects included in these estimates are detailed in Appendix C.

## Appendix C: Outlay Effects Included in Revenue Estimates

| | 2009 | 2010 | 2011 | 2012 | 2013 | 2014 | 2015 | 2016 | 2017 | 2018 | 2019 | 2010-2014 | 2010-2019 |
|---|---|---|---|---|---|---|---|---|---|---|---|---|---|
| | | | | | | (in millions of dollars) | | | | | | | |
| Make permanent the expansion of the child tax credit | 0 | 0 | 45 | 14,518 | 14,430 | 14,359 | 14,434 | 14,629 | 14,670 | 14,818 | 14,967 | 43,352 | 116,870 |
| Modify the EITC: Provide marriage penalty relief and simplify | 0 | 0 | -583 | 1,986 | 1,884 | 1,822 | 1,813 | 1,819 | 1,819 | 1,823 | 1,830 | 5,109 | 14,213 |
| Provide the making work pay tax credit | 0 | 0 | 703 | 20,749 | 20,448 | 20,214 | 20,194 | 20,267 | 20,204 | 20,239 | 20,295 | 62,114 | 163,313 |
| Expand the earned income tax credit | 0 | 0 | 0 | 2,599 | 2,536 | 2,510 | 2,547 | 2,596 | 2,644 | 2,697 | 2,755 | 7,645 | 20,884 |
| Expand the refundability of the child tax credit | 0 | 0 | 0 | 8,822 | 8,707 | 8,674 | 8,766 | 8,859 | 8,944 | 9,039 | 9,142 | 26,203 | 70,953 |
| Expand the saver's credit and provide for automatic enrollment in IRAs | 0 | 0 | 89 | 748 | 835 | 837 | 859 | 890 | 913 | 932 | 956 | 2,509 | 7,059 |
| Provide the American opportunity tax credit | 0 | 0 | 0 | 1,860 | 1,939 | 2,018 | 2,162 | 2,335 | 2,434 | 2,489 | 2,673 | 5,817 | 17,910 |
| Continue certain expiring provisions through calendar year 2010 | 0 | 62 | 21 | 0 | 0 | 0 | 0 | 0 | 0 | 0 | 0 | 83 | 83 |
| Eliminate the advanced earned income tax credit | 0 | -125 | -76 | -77 | -78 | -81 | -83 | -85 | -87 | -89 | -91 | -437 | -872 |
| **Total Outlay Effect** | **0** | **-63** | **199** | **51,205** | **50,701** | **50,353** | **50,692** | **51,310** | **51,541** | **51,948** | **52,527** | **152,395** | **410,413** |

Department of the Treasury

131